EAST ASIAN DEVELOPMENT
New Perspectives

Of Related Interest

THE STATE AND ECONOMIC DEVELOPMENT
Lessons from the Far East
edited by Robert Fitzgerald

THE COMPETITIVE ADVANTAGES OF FAR EASTERN BUSINESS
edited by Robert Fitzgerald

INTERNATIONAL COMPETITIVENESS IN LATIN AMERICA
AND EAST ASIA
by Klaus Esser, Wolfgang Hillebrand, Dirk Messner and Jorg Meyer-Stamer
(GDI Book Series No.1)

SHAPING COMPETITIVE ADVANTAGES
Conceptual Framework and the Korean Approach
by Wolfgang Hillebrand
(GDI Book Series No.6)

DEVELOPING COUNTRIES AND THE INTERNATIONAL ECONOMY
Issues in Trade, Adjustment and Debt
edited by H. David Evans and David Greenaway

SYSTEMIC COMPETITIVENESS
New Governance Patterns for Industrial Development
by Klaus Esser, Wolfgang Hillebrand, Dirk Messner and Jörg Meyer-Stamer
(GDI Book Series No.7)

GLOBALISATION, COMPETITIVENESS AND HUMAN SECURITY
edited by Cristóbal Kay

East Asian Development: New Perspectives

Edited by

Yilmaz Akyüz

Chief, Macroeconomic and Development Policies, UNCTAD

FRANK CASS
LONDON • PORTLAND, OR

First published in 1999 in Great Britain by
FRANK CASS PUBLISHERS
Newbury House, 900 Eastern Avenue,
London, IG2 7HH, England

and in the United States of America by
FRANK CASS PUBLISHERS
c/o ISBS
5804 N.E. Hassalo Street
Portland, Oregon 97213-3644

Website: http://www.frankcass.com

Copyright © 1999 Frank Cass & Co Ltd

British Library Cataloguing in Publication Data

East Asian development : new perspectives. – (Journal of
development studies ; v. 34)
1. East Asia – Economic policy 2. East Asia – Economic
conditions – 20th century
I.Akyuz, Yilmaz
338.9'5

ISBN 0 7146 4934 1 (cloth)
ISBN 0 7146 4494 3 (paper)

Library of Congress Cataloging in Publication Data

East Asian development : new perspectives / edited by Yilmaz Akyüz.
    p.   cm.
"This group of studies first appeared in a speical issue ... of
the Journal of development studies, 34/6 (August 1998) "--T.p. verso.
Includes bibliographical references and index.
ISBN 0-7146-4934-1. -- ISBN 0-7146-4494-3 (pbk.)
    1. Saving and investment--East Asia--Cass studies. 2. East Asia-
-Economic condition--Case studies. 3. East Asia--Economic policy-
-Case studies. I. Akyüz, Yilmaz.
HC460.5.Z9S33   1998
338.95--dc21   98-30180
                                                                      CIP

This group of studies first appeared in a Special Issue on
'East Asian Development: New Perspectives' of *The Journal of Development Studies*
(ISSN 0022-038) 34/6 (August 1998) published by Frank Cass.

Printed in Great Britain by
Bookcraft Ltd., Midsomer Norton, Nr Bath, Avon

Contents

Preface

Rapid growth, rising living standards and the increased international competitiveness of a small group of developing countries in East Asia have been at the centre of debates on development policy for well over a decade. The contributions in this volume are part of UNCTAD's ongoing research to explain and draw lessons from this experience. Three points emerge strongly from these studies. First, while all the East Asian countries have features in common, important differences exist among them. Second, the design of effective policies has been accompanied by institutional reforms, particularly concerning government–business relations. Third, the profit–investment–export nexus represents the central axis around which institutional reform and policy interventions have been built. Although these contributions should be read as part of a wider analysis and explanation (other aspects, particularly the role of regional trade and investment flows, have been discussed elsewhere in UNCTAD publications), it is clear that they distinguish UNCTAD's analysis from more conventional accounts of the 'East Asian Miracle'.

Since these contributions were written there has been a sea-change in attitudes towards East Asia. A deep financial crisis has swept across the region, undermining growth performance and raising serious doubts about its relevance for other developing countries. One ironic consequence of these events has been the way in which active state involvement, consistently underrated until recently by some commentators, has suddenly emerged as the main explanation for the current crisis. Many such explanations continue to ignore the region's diversity. The first-tier newly industrialising economies (NIEs) comprise one *laissez-faire* model (Hong Kong, China) and three with a more interventionist regime. Of the latter, Singapore and Taiwan Province of China have, so far, been least affected by the Asian financial crisis. By contrast, the underlying factors of the crisis appear to be far more deeply rooted in some South-East Asian countries which had until recently been perceived as placing greater reliance on market forces.

The distinction between the first- and second-tier NIEs has been central to UNCTAD's analysis of East Asia. While praising the successful policies of the second-tier NIEs which have helped establish competitive resource- and labour-intensive industries, the *Trade and Development Report 1996* pointed out that the easy stage of export promotion was coming to an end, and that those countries could suffer from loss of competitiveness. *The Report* sounded a clear warning, noting that growth in the region relied excessively on foreign resources, both labour and capital:

> Thus, the second-tier NIEs may be unable to sustain large current-account deficits over the longer term; they need to reduce their trade deficits so as to minimize the risk of serious balance of payments problems and a sharp slowdown in growth. Much will depend on their success in enhancing their export potential through upgrading ... The fact that in Malaysia and Thailand wage pressures can only be mitigated by large-scale immigration suggests that these economies may be having difficulty in achieving the necessary upgrading ... Without upgrading ... FDI will remain footloose and the economy would be highly vulnerable to interruptions of capital inflows. Concerns over such a possibility have been growing in Thailand and even more in Malaysia in view of their large current account deficits.[1]

Of course, a number of other factors have been central to the evolving financial crisis in South-East Asia.[2] Nevertheless, a combination of large current account deficits, loss of competitiveness and slowdown in exports played a major role in the crisis by triggering an attack on currencies and setting off a speculative bandwagon.

The crisis in the Republic of Korea is more complex and surprising. However, explanations in terms of dirigisme and 'crony capitalism' sound simplistic and unidimensional. A stable exchange rate, government control of external borrowing, managed competition and the coordination of private investment decisions were central to the post-war Korean success. Departure from these practices over the past few years reflects the pressures of globalisation as well as the country's graduation to industrial economy status. Nevertheless, a much more liberal stance towards business and finance has meant abandoning many of the checks and balances which had underpinned the Republic of Korea's strategic approach to integrating with the world economy, in favour of closer integration particularly with global financial markets. This appears to have been part of the problem rather the required solution, given the systemic deficiencies and inherent instability of these markets.

Speculation about the region's future prospects is not helpful. Certainly, growth will falter this year, but over the longer term much will depend on how the crisis is managed and the response of the international community. The latter in particular can play a crucial role in determining whether the countries concerned will be able to export and grow out of the crisis, or will encounter protectionist pressures and financial stringency, undergoing prolonged stagnation, as was the case in Latin America in the 1980s.

Understanding these recent developments in East Asia and linking them to the future direction of the world economy and systemic shortcomings of international finance form the basis of ongoing research in UNCTAD.

The contributions in this volume have been prepared as part of the project on 'East Asian Development: Lessons for a New Global Environment' and extend UNCTAD's research on East Asia begun in the *Trade and Development Report 1994*. They were among a number of studies that provided the background for a conference held in Kuala Lumpur in spring 1996, attended by some 80 policy-makers, academics and senior economists from various regions. The project was directed by Yilmaz Akyüz, Chief, Macroeconomic and Development Policies, and the research was coordinated by Richard Kozul-Wright of the same unit and Ha-Joon Chang of the University of Cambridge, United Kingdom. We would very much like to thank the government of Japan, which generously made available funds for this project from the Japan Trust Fund for International Cooperation for Development, and we hope that the collaborative efforts reflected in the contributions in this volume and involving UNCTAD staff members, outside academic experts and government policy-makers will help to improve the development dialogue to which UNCTAD is committed.

RUBENS RICUPERO
Secretary-General of UNCTAD
March 1998

NOTES

1. *Trade and Development Report 1996*, UNCTAD, Geneva, pp.102 and 123.
2. See *Trade and Development Report 1998*, UNCTAD, Geneva.

New Perspectives on East Asian Development

YILMAZ AKYÜZ, HA-JOON CHANG and RICHARD KOZUL-WRIGHT

Conventional explanations of rapid growth in East Asia have focused on the efficient allocation of resources resulting from market-led outward-oriented strategies. This study challenges that approach. East Asian success has centred around the accumulation dynamic both because of its direct importance to the growth process and also because of its close and interdependent linkages with exports. On this basis the study considers the institutions and policies which were used to manage economic rents in support of rapid growth and to ensure a more strategic and orderly integration into the world economy. The study also examines the contribution of regional trade and investment flows to East Asian industrialisation. The potential for replicating similar strategies is considered.

INTRODUCTION

Rapid growth, rising living standards and increased international competitiveness in the economies of East Asia have caught the attention of policy-makers and researchers in other developing regions, as well as in the developed world, opening a broad discussion on the lessons that can be drawn for meeting the wider challenges of economic development. However, how such high and sustained rates of growth have been achieved

Yilmaz Akyüz and Richard Kozul-Wright, United Nations Conference on Trade and Development (UNCTAD), Geneva, Switzerland; Ha-Joon Chang, Faculty of Economics and Politics, University of Cambridge, United Kingdom. The opinions expressed in this contribution and the designations and terminology used are those of the authors and do not necessarily reflect the views of UNCTAD. The work of colleagues, particularly Detlef Kotte, Murray Gibbs and Bob Rowthorn, in shaping this paper is gratefully acknowledged. Final responsibility rests with the authors.

among a large group of economies is still the subject of considerable debate.[1]

Initially, the East Asian experience was seen as vindicating a market-based industrialisation strategy.[2] From this perspective, the first wave of successful industrialisation in East Asia emerged with the rapid dismantling of government restrictions in the immediate post-war period, allowing the private sector to operate freely under world market prices. Similar measures repeated subsequently have created new waves of industrialisation across the region, enabling East Asian development to approximate a regime of *laissez-faire*, where higher rates of growth have been achieved through greater allocative efficiency, especially gains from international trade, resulting from the exploitation of comparative advantages and greater competition.

Some cracks started to appear in this view in the early 1980s. The graduation of Japan to economic superpower prompted an intense debate on the causes of its industrial strength – a debate centred, to a large extent, on the role of selective industrial policy.[3] At much the same time, more detailed studies of the first-tier NIEs showed that these countries were also using a range of interventions to channel resources from old into new industries, altering their long-term development trajectory.[4] These interpretations of East Asian development offered a cogent critique of the more conventional perspective focusing on the role of state intervention in late industrializing economies.

Recently, a more rounded position has been offered by the World Bank in its *East Asian Miracle* [*World Bank, 1993*].[5] This study traces what it variously calls a 'market-friendly' or 'market-conforming' chain of causation in East Asia from greater competition and rapidly improving educational levels to the promotion of technical progress, total factor productivity (TFP) growth and hence economic expansion. Measures aimed at the free mobility of labour, capital and technology, and the free entry and exit of firms are regarded as having played a crucial role in the spread of knowledge and technical change in East Asia. However, in this perspective the 'public' qualities of knowledge and technology allow a larger role for the state than in the earlier free-market interpretations of East Asian development, including a possible role for more selective interventions, particularly in financial and labour markets.

But while the World Bank study provides a wealth of detail on the performance of these high-growth economies and has gone further in acknowledging the positive contribution of government policy in some rapidly industrialising economies, it has largely failed to carry the development debate beyond traditional dichotomies counterposing the state and market, and export-oriented and import substitution industrialisation strategies. In part, this reflects the reluctance of the mainstream economists to integrate the findings of more heterodox economists. But it also reflects their unwillingness, shared to various degrees by many other contributors to the debate, to break with a conventional focus on the allocation of resources and sectoral growth patterns.

Advancing the discussion of East Asia now requires a shift in thinking. By way of an introduction, this paper offers an overview of the East Asian experience centred on the role of capital accumulation in the process of rapid industrialisation. More particularly, and to avoid the mistakes of replacing one all-encompassing type of explanation with another, the next section introduces the concepts of the 'profit–investment nexus' and 'export–investment nexus' to highlight the interdependence of key elements in the industrialisation process in East Asia. This is followed by a discussion of the politics of rapid investment, and in particular the kinds of institutions and policies used successfully in East Asia to manage economic rents. The next sections consider similarities and differences in the industrialisation experience of the East Asian NIEs, as well as the role of a wider regional dynamic. A final section considers to what extent changes in the world economy over the past decade have overtaken this experience as a useful one for other developing countries to follow.

I. THE EAST ASIAN DEVELOPMENT EXPERIENCE

(1) One or Many East Asian Models?

The general features of East Asian development are well known; fast economic growth over three decades has been accompanied by a very rapid pace of capital accumulation and a strong rise in exports as a share of output, which together have helped shift the dynamic fulcrum of the economy towards industrial activity. While this strong economic performance suggests a shared experience among countries in the region, there has been a growing awareness of differences among the countries of East Asia in terms of the specific policies and institutions used to accelerate industrialisation and achieve rapid economic growth.

The size and non-rural economic structure have been distinct influences on the scope of industrial diversification, reliance on FDI and infrastructural needs in Hong Kong and Singapore.[6] But striking institutional and structural differences also exist among the three economies whose development paths share the closest resemblance, namely Japan, Korea and Taiwan. For example, the conflict between the Kuomintang Government and the descendants of those who migrated from the mainland centuries earlier not only acted as a restraint on the growth of large firms in the private sector but also contributed to a large state-owned sector in Taiwan [*Field, 1995*]. Korea, by contrast, has developed a much more centralised economic bureaucracy, which has not only strongly favoured the development of large, diversified, private conglomerates, but also allowed the state to engage in more ambitious industrial policies than those implemented in Taiwan or, indeed, in Japan. To take another example, the relative strength of the business community has made it necessary for the Japanese Government to take a more consultative approach in its dealings with the private sector through active use of deliberation councils and industrial associations than has been the case in Korea or Taiwan.[7]

More recently, it has become popular to distinguish a South-East Asian development model, different from the one followed by the North-East Asian countries (Japan and the first-tier NIEs, excepting Hong Kong). In particular, it is claimed that the South-East Asian NIEs have adopted a much less demanding policy regime, which relies less on interventionist industrial policies and more on conservative macroeconomic management, as well as liberal trade and FDI policies. On these grounds, the South-East Asian model is often recommended to other developing countries as easier to imitate [*World Bank, 1993*]. We shall consider this contrast between North-East and South-East Asia in greater detail later in this study. But it is first necessary, in light of both their strong performance over a number of decades and the recognition of differences among them, to identify common principles behind rapid growth and industrialisation in Japan and the first-tier NIEs.[8]

(2) Common Principles Behind North-East Asia's Development Experiences

The profit–investment nexus: Any long-run rise in living standards can only be achieved through sustained productivity growth. This in turn presupposes high rates of investment in plant and equipment and physical infrastructure, as well as in more intangible elements, such as education and research and development. After something of a hiatus in the development literature, the role of capital accumulation in the process of rapid growth is once again gaining attention [*De Long and Summers, 1991; Schmidt-Hebbel et al., 1996*]. There is little doubting East Asian success in these respects. Controversy, however, concerns the way in which high rates of investment have been achieved.

Conventional analysis offers very little explanation for the rapid and unprecedented rise in savings and investments in Japan and the first-tier NIEs from their very low levels in the 1950s, but emphasises stable macroeconomic conditions and 'getting the fundamentals right' by opening the economy to world market forces in improving both allocative and productive efficiency.[9] Productivity growth is, in this view, essentially the outcome of allowing markets to operate freely to the fullest possible extent; hence the call for rapid domestic liberalisation and full integration with the world economy.[10] There are two basic problems with this approach. First, it assumes that the level and structure of investment will be optimally guided by price signals. This tends to downplay the many problems which arise from the fact that investment involves an irreversible commitment of resources to an uncertain future where price signals are, at best, imperfect signals and waiting strategies can forestall long-term investment commitments. Secondly, it ignores the strong complementarities between investment and other aspects of the growth process, including exports and technological progress, which can give rise to a very high social return to investment. But if dynamic externalities linked to scale economies and learning require effective linkages between these complementary aspects of industrialisation and growth, where these do not emerge spontaneously effective policy initiatives must supplement or replace market forces.

All the North-East Asian governments tried to guarantee certain basic conditions for investment by maintaining political stability and creating a 'pro-investment' macroeconomic climate. Pro-investment is a better description of East Asian macroeconomic policies than stable or low-inflationary, because some of these governments were willing to tolerate a fair degree of inflationary pressure for the sake of boosting investors' confidence. Moreover, consumption rather than investment was sacrificed first when more restrictive measures were seen as necessary to balance national economic goals.

But, in addition, strong incentives were provided to encourage investment by introducing measures to boost profits above their free-market levels. This was done in two ways.[11] A range of fiscal instruments was used to supplement corporate profits and to encourage their retention in order to accelerate capital accumulation; tax exemptions and special depreciation allowances were applied both on a general level as well as targeted at specific industries. But trade, financial and competition policies were also used to create 'rents' that boosted corporate profits and therefore the potential investible resources available to corporations. This included a mix of selective policies of protection, controls over interest rates and credit allocation, and managed competition, including the encouragement of mergers, the coordination of capacity expansion, restrictions on entry into specific industries, screening of technology acquisition, and the promotion of cartels for specific purposes such as standardisation, specialisation and exports. As a result of these measures, corporate savings came to play a particularly important role in boosting capital accumulation.

However, policy-makers in these countries did not believe that channelling resources into the hands of potential investors was enough. In their view, there was no guarantee that corporations would use such resources for productive investment purposes, or that all investments would in the long run sustain rapid productivity growth. To begin with, potential investors could use the resources made available to them simply to increase luxury consumption – a possibility that seems to have materialised after the recent liberalisation episodes in Latin America [*UNCTAD, 1996*]. In order to prevent this, the East Asian economies put severe restrictions on luxury consumption [*UNCTAD, 1997: 179-82*], both directly through restricting the import and domestic production of luxury consumption goods, and indirectly through high taxation and restrictions on consumer credits, although the mix of measures differed across countries.

The East Asian governments also tried to eliminate speculative investment opportunities. It is generally accepted that investments aimed at an arbitrage gain, even if they increase short-term efficiency, may have only limited positive, and even harmful, effects on long-run productivity growth. In particular, the high and quick returns associated with risky speculative investments are unlikely to be compatible with the kind of 'animal spirits' necessary for more productive investments. In this context, a related group of measures used to sustain high levels of productive investments in East Asia involved restrictions on the outflow of capital during the initial stages of their development.[12]

Together this mixture of incentives and disciplinary measures has created and sustained a dynamic profit–investment nexus in East Asia [*Akyüz and Gore, 1996*]; high profits have increased simultaneously the incentive of firms to invest, and their capacity to finance new, higher, investment has in turn raised profits by enhancing both the rates of capital utilisation and the pace of productivity growth.

The export–investment nexus: The challenge of economic development does not end with achieving high levels of investment. Even if all the resources mobilised are invested productively, there is still ground for asking whether they are being invested in the 'right' areas. Answering this question has often been obscured by arguments about the effectiveness of industrial policy in countries at a more advanced stage of economic development. Unlike developed countries, developing countries are not initially operating at the technological frontier of international best practice. Consequently, promoting industrial development does not involve their 'picking winners' in an uncertain technological race based on innovation, but lifting the propensity to invest and promoting movements along existing learning curves, including learning how to acquire mastery over readily available technologies and how to compete in mature-product markets with already established firms. In this respect, an important feature of East Asian development has been efforts to link the profit–investment nexus to the export–investment nexus.

A large part of the theoretical rationale for exports emphasises efficiency gains. Increasingly, this has been linked to the disciplining effect of international competition as much as to the optimal signalling properties of international prices. However, in practice perhaps the most important factor underlying an export drive in developing countries has come from the need to overcome the balance-of-payments constraint on rapid economic growth.[13] In building up their industrial capacity and competitive strength, all newly industrialising countries must import a large volume of capital goods and intermediate goods. Thus, in an economy where investment is growing both in absolute terms and as a proportion of GDP, such imports will also need to grow faster than GDP, and the financing of these imports may pose a serious constraint on the industrialisation process if additional export revenue cannot be obtained. This is not a one-off challenge. Even if domestic industries producing capital goods and intermediate inputs are gradually established to meet the demands of the first generation of industries, as the economy moves up the technological ladder and establishes new industries and product lines, it will continue to require a considerable volume of imported capital goods and intermediate inputs. While the speed at which a domestic capital goods industry is established, develops and becomes internationally competitive has a critical influence on the balance-of-payments constraint, it still remains true that the faster is the pace of this upgrading and technological advance, the greater the likely dependence on such imports.

Export of manufactures is not the only means of meeting the import bill. Primary export earnings as well as external borrowing, grants by foreign governments, inflows of FDI or worker remittances from abroad can also provide the foreign exchange needed.[14]

An economy which is poor in natural resources, as is the case in North-East Asia, cannot rely on the growth of primary export earnings to meet the growing import bill of the industrial sector. In any case, there are often limits to raising productivity and exports in the primary sector, so that even in countries rich in natural resources it would eventually be necessary to expand exports of manufactures. On the other hand, in the absence of rising export earnings, increased external borrowing would raise the debt-service ratio, thereby making it difficult to maintain capital inflows. Under such circumstances, expansion of manufacturing exports appears to be the only way of sustaining the momentum of industrialisation right from the early stages of development.

There is yet another aspect of the relation between exports and industrialisation which has received little attention in the literature. While it is possible to raise investment without increasing manufacturing exports, an economy without a significant capital goods industry cannot increase its domestic savings without exporting. In the absence of exports, industry will have to rely on domestic demand to sell the goods it produces. When the output of the industry consists mainly of consumer goods, as is usually the case in a typical developing country, the only way to maintain a high rate of capacity utilisation is through expansion of domestic consumer demand. If there is no domestic consumer demand, goods will not be produced, and if goods are not produced, incomes and therefore savings will be correspondingly lower. But if they are produced to meet consumption demand, this also means that they are not being saved.

It is true that expansion of domestic consumption demand could provide an incentive for new investment, and the imports needed may be financed by inflows of foreign exchange through channels other than exports so that the economy can grow without an increase in domestic savings (see the contribution by You in this volume). However, as the Latin American experience shows, such a process is not sustainable; if the outlet for the rising volume of consumer goods produced with the additional capacity continuously comes from increased domestic consumer demand, domestic savings will, correspondingly, be lower and the balance-of-payments constraint will be reached more quickly.

Needless to say, while exports are necessary to raise domestic savings, they are not sufficient, since export earnings can also be used to import consumer goods or inputs into domestic consumer industries. In other words, increases in exports not associated with increases in domestic savings will not translate into investment and growth.

In sum, these considerations suggest that for growth to be sustained exports need to expand, allowing domestic industry to operate at full capacity without relying solely on domestic consumer demand, and providing the necessary balance-of-payments financing for imports of capital goods. But since export expansion in turn depends on the creation of additional production capacity in industry as well as productivity growth which is dependent upon new investment, a sustainable growth process requires mutually reinforcing dynamic interactions among savings, exports and investment. Such a process will be characterised by continuously rising exports, domestic savings and investment, both in absolute terms and, for most part of the industrialisation process, as a proportion of GDP. Initially, investment is likely to exceed domestic savings by a large margin, with the difference being financed by net inflows of capital, but over time the external gap should narrow as exports and savings grow faster than investment.

TABLE 1
GROSS NATIONAL SAVINGS, GROSS DOMESTIC INVESTMENT AND EXPORTS IN
THE ASIAN NIEs, 1951–94
(Percentage of GDP)

Country	Period	Savings	Investment	Exports
Republic of Korea	1951–1960	3.3	10.0	2.0
	1961–1970	13.7	20.0	9.1
	1971–1980	22.0	28.0	27.6
	1981–1990	30.4	30.7	35.4
	1991–1994	34.7	37.1	28.6
Taiwan	1951–1960	9.8	16.3	9.6
Province of China	1961–1970	19.7	21.9	20.4
	1971–1980	31.9	30.5	46.4
	1981–1990	32.9	21.9	53.5
	1991–1994	27.4	23.2	46.1
Hong Kong	1951–1960	9.2	9.1	–
	1961–1970	20.6	20.6	–
	1971–1980	28.3	26.7	–
	1981–1990	34.0	24.8	–
	1991–1994	34.0	27.6	–
Singapore	1951–1960	–	11.4[a]	–
	1961–1970	14.9	22.3	–
	1971–1980	28.9	41.2	–
	1981–1990	42.1	42.1	–
	1991–1994	48.9	36.3	–
Indonesia	1951–1960	–	9.2[a]	13.6[a]
	1961–1970	4.9	10.4	9.7
	1971–1980	24.6	22.7	23.6
	1981–1990	25.1	28.3	24.6
	1991–1994	26.9	29.7	27.0
Malaysia	1951–1960	23.2[b]	15.3[a]	51.4[a]
	1961–1970	21.5[c]	19.9	42.3
	1971–1980	26.2	26.3	46.4
	1981–1990	27.4	30.7	60.1
	1991–1994	30.0	36.1	82.7
Thailand	1961–1960	15.3	13.5	18.3
	1961–1970	19.9	21.5	16.2
	1971–1980	22.4	26.2	20.0
	1981–1990	26.2	30.7	26.8
	1991–1994	33.7	40.5	36.9

Source: UNCTAD data base.

Notes: Exports include services.
a = 1960 only.
b = Including Singapore, which became independent in 1965.
c = 1965–70.

The evolution of investment, savings and exports in all the first-tier NIEs during the past three decades corresponds closely to this pattern of rapid sustainable growth (Table 1). Accelerating accumulation began in the 1950s and rose continuously until the 1980s, when (with the exception of Korea) it stagnated before picking up again in the 1990s. Initially, import substitution industries emerged in activities where local resources, including labour, could be quickly mobilised and where domestic demand could be generated. In most cases, the export–investment nexus was built around these same traditional low-skill industries. However, the emergence of successful export-oriented industries does not follow spontaneously from rapid capital accumulation. Indeed, there is plenty of evidence to suggest that a switch to manufactured exports if not properly managed can very easily get stuck [*Hirschman, 1995: 2; UNCTAD, 1992*] In this respect, two features of the export-investment nexus in Korea and Taiwan need to be considered; first, the pace at which export growth of labour-intensive manufactures was achieved; secondly the capacity to upgrade their industrial structure.

As in most developing countries, primary exports were the initial source of foreign exchange earnings in Korea and Taiwan in the early 1950s. Also, as in many other developing countries at that time, efforts were made from an early date to move into manufactured goods, initially in wood and paper products, more significantly, and, as was earlier the case in Hong Kong, in textiles and clothing. In both Korea and Taiwan, labour-intensive exports as a share of their domestic production rose continuously and rapidly from the mid-1960s, reaching 60 per cent in the early 1980s.[15] In line with these countries' expansion of low-skill labour-intensive manufacturing, the shares of primary commodities in total exports fell rapidly; by 1975 these accounted for 18 per cent in Korea and 20 per cent in Taiwan (Table 2).

Although these countries enjoyed a comparative advantage in labour-intensive manufacturing industries, this did not mean that investments in these industries were automatically forthcoming. In most cases, they still needed government support in financing, international marketing, and sometimes even export subsidies in order to become viable in the world market. Nevertheless, it is true that the development of these industries was largely based on encouraging productive investments, and that at this stage the East Asian countries were not as extensively engaged in a selective industrial policy as they were at a later stage. However, even if investments are made in industries with static comparative advantages arising from existing resource endowments, including labour, constraints on the room for productivity growth means that rising domestic wages and loss of competitiveness can quickly bring a halt to an export drive. In anticipation of such potential difficulties, East Asian economies, from the early stages of

TABLE 2
PRIMARY COMMODITIES AND LABOUR-INTENSIVE AND RESOURCE-BASED
EXPORTS AS A SHARE OF TOTAL NON-OIL EXPORTS OF SELECTED
DEVELOPING COUNTRIES AND REGIONS, 1965–94

	First-tier NIEs (2 countries)[a]	Second-tier NIEs	Latin America (3 countries)[b]	Brazil	Mexico
Primary commodities[c]					
1965	51.4	96.6	94.6	92.3	84.3
1975	18.4	87.5	81.6	74.0	64.8
1985	7.2	67.6	84.0	52.8	33.9
1994	6.1	31.4	69.5	43.9	13.1
Primary commodities[c] plus resource-based and low-skill labour-intensive goods[d]					
1965	86.5	97.7	96.6	94.2	89.2
1975	69.4	93.2	87.7	83.4	75.0
1985	47.6	82.9	89.6	64.1	44.7
1994	31.6	59.0	82.0	58.1	22.8

Source: UNCTAD data base.

Notes: a = Republic of Korea and Taiwan Province of China.
b = Argentina, Chile and Colombia.
c = Excluding petroleum and including non-ferrous metals (SITC 68).
d = Wood and paper products; non-metallic mineral products; textiles and clothing (including footwear); and toys and sports equipment.

their development, gradually and purposefully nurtured new generations of industries with a greater potential for innovation, exporting and productivity growth in the long run.

Thus, in these countries measures to promote investment were linked to the establishment of domestic capital and intermediate goods industries and technological upgrading. These included re-instituting import restrictions, rolling back tax exemptions on the import of certain intermediate and capital goods and granting higher investment tax credits to businesses purchasing domestically produced machinery. In addition, a policy was pursued of building up a technological capacity at the national, industry and even firm levels. In these economies, tax and other incentives for enterprise training were complemented by a more detailed national training programme, which placed greater emphasis on technical subjects at higher levels of education and on greater industry involvement in vocational training schemes. Measures to facilitate local R&D, including direct financial subsidies, have also been extensively used.

Given that technological and organisational leadership was located abroad, the transfer and adaptation of foreign technology was, from an early stage, recognised by policy-makers in East Asia as a critical link in the process of industrial upgrading. Acquiring new technologies required generating foreign exchange, and it was for this purpose, as well as to provide an outlet for industrial production without promoting domestic consumption, and to expose the recipients of rents to a measured degree of competition on world markets, that East Asian governments encouraged exports. As a result of these various policy initiatives, the first-tier NIEs have been particularly successful in upgrading their structure of manufacturing output towards scale- and skill-intensive activities. By the second half of the 1980s, the share of these activities in total manufacturing output had passed that of resource and labour-intensive activities. The rising share of these scale- and skill-intensive goods in total manufacturing exports (although initially lagging in their share of total output) also began to accelerate rapidly from the mid-1970s. These goods not only comprise the majority of manufactured exports from the first-tier NIEs but have also gained substantial shares in world markets [*UNCTAD, 1996*].

Despite a strong export-orientation, the East Asian economies were not from their early stages of development fully integrated with the world economy. Rather, integration was strategic, tailored to specific sectoral needs and their level of industrial and economic development, and sequenced accordingly [*Singh, 1995*]. Moreover, strategic integration was not only confined to trade relations but also extended to technology transfer. At the aggregate national level, FDI has not been a significant factor in Japan, Korea or Taiwan, although playing a larger role in Hong Kong and in particular Singapore (Table 3). In the first group of economies in sectors where FDI has played a significant role, for example, textiles and electronics, government policy has been a major influence, promoting joint ventures, screening imported technologies and bargaining over local content agreements, and in the process firmly embedding transnational corporations (TNCs) in a national industrialisation strategy.[16]

Managing economic rents: Building an export–investment nexus alongside a strong profit–investment nexus in East Asia has not involved unfamiliar policy measures. However, the deliberate creation of rents for infant industries implied by many of these measures has produced less desirable results elsewhere. Not only does the creation of rents mean a sacrifice in current income and the transfer of resources to activities with more uncertain prospects, but there is a real danger with this strategy that rents, unless properly managed, can become more permanent, in the long run weakening entrepreneurship and hampering productivity growth [*Chang, 1994*].

East Asian governments have solved these potential problems in two

TABLE 3
RATIO OF FDI INFLOWS TO GROSS FIXED CAPITAL FORMATION
IN SELECTED EAST ASIAN COUNTRIES, 1971–93
(Percentage)

Country	1971–1980	1981–1990	1991–1993
Japan	0.1	0.1	0.1
Hong Kong	5.1	9.9	5.7
Republic of Korea	1.2	0.9	0.5
Singapore	15.8	26.2	37.4
Taiwan Province of China	1.3	2.6	2.6
Indonesia	3.5	1.5	4.5
Malaysia	13.6	11.3	24.6
Philippines	1.0	3.8	4.6
Thailand	2.3	4.8	5.0
China	0.0	1.5	10.4

Source: UNCTAD data base.

ways. First, they established policy mechanisms and institutions to ensure that creating the initial rents was essentially a 'priming' exercise and that the rents would eventually be withdrawn as the industry matured. Secondly, they imposed performance criteria on the recipients of the rents, in particular by using the discipline of the international market, through for example export targets – a process sometimes described as establishing 'contests' [*World Bank, 1993*]. As pointed out earlier, infant industries promoted through state-created rents were expected to eventually prove themselves by the standards of the international market, and had their import protection gradually removed and/or were pushed by the government to start exporting at a relatively earlier stage of development. Such an imperative exercised a powerful market-based discipline on the recipients of rents.

Behind this successful management of economic rents in East Asia lies a much deeper process of building a robust network of government and business institutions consistent with strategic development goals. On the one hand, this has involved the creation of a strong meritocratic civil service able to attract high-calibre bureaucrats, and with long-term organisational goals that are not unduly burdened with immediate political concerns (see section III (2) below). On the other hand, it has involved creating a series of formal and informal links with the entrepreneurial classes to assist in the design, implementation and coordination of policy measures, including sector-specific agencies within existing bureaucracies or the creation of specialised sector-specific institutions. Significantly, as the contributions by Evans and Haggard *et al.* in this volume show, in the cases of both Korea and Taiwan close relations with business were not inherited from the pre-industrial era but evolved along with the process of industrial development itself.

But North-East Asian success cannot be attributed exclusively to the effective design and implementation of policies by a developmental state. Just as important has been the evolution and organisation of a domestic entrepreneurial class. As the contribution by Singh shows, in this respect, an important feature of the management of economic rents in East Asia has been the emergence of large diversified corporations. These firms (*keiretsus* in Japan and *chaebols* in Korea) have been able to establish a pattern of corporate governance which has protected their investment strategy from short-term profit goals and has successfully coordinated activities across a number of industries. Although in Taiwan such organisational structures have been less prominent, large state-owned enterprises have played an important coordinating role [*Amsden, 1991; Field, 1995*].

One particularly important feature of these business links has been in the financial sector. Failures on the capital markets caused by information imperfections and coordination problems are recognised to pose a major obstacle to rapid investment and innovation, particularly in developing countries, where risks are high [*Stiglitz, 1994; Studart, 1995*]. The socialisation of risk through bank-based lending has provided the means of overcoming these problems, and a variety of institutional links between corporations and banks have been devised to ensure a better investment regime [*Akyüz, 1993*]. In East Asia this has also been an important focus for government-business collaboration, either through state-owned banks or considerable state direction of the financial sector [*UNCTAD, 1994; Stiglitz and Uy, 1996*].

As noted earlier, the management of economic rents cannot be viewed as a harmonious process. Rather it carries direct implications for the distribution of income and can give rise to distributional conflicts which can quite quickly undermine a sustainable growth path. On some accounts of East Asian success, a favourable income distribution has been a prerequisite of its rapid growth by providing a more stable investment climate. However, the analysis by You suggests a rather more uneven picture of income distribution across the region as a whole, with only Korea and Taiwan exhibiting an exemplary pattern of income distribution and growth. Moreover, while favourable initial conditions, particularly land reform, provide one important explanation of this pattern, this does not suggest why this situation has persisted over time with very fast rates of investment and high profits. Rather the answer appears to lie in the institutional and policy factors which lie behind a dynamic profit–investment nexus.

II. THE REGIONAL CONTEXT

(1) North-East Asia and South-East Asia: How Different from Each Other?

The previous section identified a number of common elements from North-East Asian development experience and their interrelationship. A general impression of the second-tier South-East Asian NIEs is that their success has rested on different principles. In particular, it has been argued that their export orientation is more closely tied to a liberal policy environment, is more dependent upon FDI, and has involved minimal industrial policy. This has been taken to signal their much fuller and less selective integration with the world economy – and as a model for other developing economies to follow.

Two general points should be borne in mind when looking for similarities and differences between the region's early and later industrialisers. Firstly, when discussing the particularly rapid growth of the second-tier NIEs over the past decade, it is often forgotten that, taking a longer perspective, there has been a significant performance gap between them and the first-tier NIEs. Although the exact result will depend on which periods and which countries are being observed, the annual per capita GDP growth rates of Japan and the first-tier NIEs have, on average, been roughly two percentage points higher than those of the second-tier NIEs over the past three decades or so. The cumulative impact of this growth gap is significant. In 1961, Korea's per capita income (in current dollars) was somewhat lower than that of Thailand; it is now three and a half times higher. Even more striking, Malaysia's per capita income was almost three times that of Korea and almost twice that of Taiwan in 1961 (Malaysia then included Singapore, so purely 'Malaysian' income would have been somewhat lower), remained higher than that of Korea until 1981, but in 1993 was less than half that of Korea, and about one third that of Taiwan.

Secondly, these differing growth dynamics can, in part, be explained by differences with respect to resource endowments. Unlike the economies of South East Asia, the North-East Asian economies lacked abundant natural resources. This was an important factor behind their rapid shift to manufactured exports. In contrast, the natural resource wealth of Indonesia, Malaysia and Thailand gave rise to agro-based leading sectors, which could become competitive on world markets with a more modest initial role for the government and less dependence on imported inputs. In recent decades, these sectors have accounted for much of the growth in South East Asia, and of their exports in particular. This also, in part, explains why upgrading has been much slower than in the first-tier NIEs (Table 2).

However, such differences do not exclude similarities in the development experience of the two groups of countries. The most obvious point of similarity is the pace of investment. Gross domestic investment as a share of GDP has risen continuously in all three South-East Asian NIEs over the past two decades. Malaysia was first to experience a rapid acceleration in capital formation, beginning in the early 1970s, but Indonesia and Thailand have both experienced particularly rapid rates of investment since the early 1980s; by the early 1990s, gross domestic investment was over 30 per cent of GDP in all three countries, and has continued to rise in the 1990s (Table 1).

In this context, it is possible to identify similar policy measures used to establish a dynamic profit-investment nexus, including favourable fiscal measures and the deliberate creation of rents. Many of these measures were first employed in agriculture; public investment in agricultural infrastructure and services, favourable incentives, including subsidised credits, and agricultural research have played an important role in facilitating investment in agriculture and improving productivity. In Thailand, in the 1950s and 1960s, for example, investment funds were channelled into infrastructure to open up more cultivated land, investment incentives were mainly offered to agro-business and the government intervened to increase the credit available to crop growers and exporters. Indonesia's impressive growth in agricultural output over the past three decades has similarly been based on massive investment in agricultural infrastructure, large fertiliser subsidies and strong government direction.[17] Again, as in the first-tier NIEs, labour-intensive export-oriented manufacturing did not develop spontaneously through the availability of cheap labour and free trade. Besides the provision of infrastructure and primary education, direct incentives, including tax breaks and subsidies, support for training and export promotion measures have been used extensively to accelerate investment in these industries and to exploit their comparative advantages.

However, the exact form taken by the profit-investment nexus has been different in individual countries in South-East Asia. Both Thailand and Indonesia used tax exemptions, tariff protection and subsidised credit to favour the development of large domestic firms along the lines pursued earlier by Korea. In Thailand, informal links between privately owned banks and large domestic firms played a particularly important role in this process. In Indonesia more *ad hoc* government measures, including officially sanctioned cartels, price controls, exclusive licensing and public-sector monopolies, were used in support of specific industrial business groups. The situation has been more complex in Malaysia: selective targeting and generous fiscal incentives have favoured large foreign-owned firms in some industries and state-owned enterprises in others, alongside measures to encourage the development of small and medium-sized firms among local entrepreneurs. Measures have also been taken to discipline the recipients of rents through restrictions on luxury consumption and efforts to curtail speculative investments.

Although their rich natural resource endowments allowed the second-tier NIEs to pursue a long period of import-substitution industrialisation, limits on the growth potential of this process became apparent in the 1970s and early 1980s, and provoked a series of policy reforms subjecting domestic producers to the greater influence of international market pressures. In this context, the second-tier NIEs have been more willing to allow in wholly-owned foreign subsidiaries and have taken a less restrictive approach to FDI than some of the first-tier NIEs to compensate for the absence of local entrepreneurial and organisational skills, capital, technological capacity and international marketing networks. More liberal foreign investment laws were introduced, or their implementation accelerated, in the 1980s – a period which coincided with a sharp shift in the competitive position of firms in both Japan and the first-tier NIEs [*Akyüz, 1997*].

However, contrary to much conventional wisdom, only Malaysia among the second-tier NIEs has been exceptionally dependent on FDI by developing country standards (Table 3). Moreover, while industrial policies in the South-East Asian countries may not have been used as systematically as by their North-Eastern counterparts, they have, in all cases, been part of the policy agenda. Nor is it true that all such policies were misconceived or have failed [*Jomo et al., 1997*]. The Malaysian attempt at strategic industrial policy, for example, did have some success in certain industries, especially following the adoption of the Industrial Master Plan in the mid-1980s, which strengthened incentives for technological deepening and domestic sourcing of inputs in strategic firms, sought to strengthen linkages between foreign and domestic firms, and introduced more advanced infant industry protection. Indonesia built up an important wing of the bureaucracy devoted to developing advanced industries, such as aviation, automobiles, steel and shipbuilding. Thailand, while less inclined to large-scale projects, has rather successfully used tariff protection and other measures to promote some selected industries.

Nevertheless, to date this mix of influences has not created the pattern of industrial upgrading already found in the first-tier NIEs. Although Malaysia and Thailand, through their reliance on FDI, have succeeded in high technology exports, which in large part combine low-skill assembly activities with high-technology imported parts, both countries have yet to develop a diversified manufacturing base. In particular, their early orientation towards electronics contrasts with the slow development of most capital goods industries, such as iron and steel, non-electrical machinery, metal products and transport equipment. The continued heavy reliance on imports of both capital and intermediate goods suggests that the second-tier NIEs have still to embark on the kind of upgrading process in the medium technology sectors pursued earlier by the first-tier NIEs. Many of the elements of the technological infrastructure needed to allow domestic firms to compete in this middle range of exports are still missing. These countries have still to put in place a well-developed local supplier network, incipient clusters of high-technology activities and an adequately trained workforce; nor do they have any significant industrial R&D, either within the enterprise system or in the public sector. In the absence of these linkages, local firms in key sectors such as electronics continue to concentrate on the supply of secondary materials and services, such as packaging and transportation.

The lack of comprehensive and integrated industrial policies, as well as of adequate manpower planning and other related policies to widen and deepen the skill base of the economy, also casts some doubts about the medium-term industrial upgrading of these countries. The fact that Malaysia and Thailand are currently experiencing large-scale immigration to fight the wage pressures – something that only began in the North-East Asian economies at a much higher level of income – suggests that these economies may be having difficulty in achieving the necessary upgrading. Furthermore, Malaysia's high reliance on FDI is raising concerns about a dualistic economic structure with insufficient technological and supply links between the TNC-dominated export sectors and the domestic economy. Just as worrying is that the limited product diversification of the export sector, the predominance of simple assembly and finishing operations and the low level of technological capabilities in this sector have given rise to the fear that China, Viet Nam and other lower-wage Asian countries could take away these sources of growth momentum, unless measures are introduced to deepen the domestic industrial base and improve the quality of workers, managers and infrastructure in line with rising production costs. The footloose character of FDI and the difficulties in sustaining the pace of export growth have been giving rise to serious concerns over the longer-term growth prospects of these countries, particularly in view of their large current account deficits and vulnerability to interruption of capital inflows.[18]

On the positive side, the South-East Asian countries continue to maintain relatively high levels of domestic savings as well as high levels of investment, which are a prerequisite for upgrading. Moreover, the key features of the export–investment nexus are also in place. There are also clear signs that Malaysia and Thailand have recently become more interested in strategic industrial policy in order to move to more technologically demanding industries as their economies began to feel the limits of static comparative advantage.

(2) Regional Dynamics

The success of Japan, closely followed by the first-tier NIEs, first focused attention on the East Asia region as a new growth pole in the world economy. More recently, the rapid growth of the second-tier NIEs and the re-emergence of China and Viet Nam have added weight to the idea of a wave of industrial development spreading across a much wider region. This regional concentration of newly industrialising economies has suggested, to some observers, a close association between the pattern of industrialisation and its regional location. In particular, the upgrading of economic activity from resource-based and labour-intensive industries to more and more sophisticated manufactures by the lead economies has opened up opportunities for less developed countries to enter the regional division of labour by picking up less demanding activities. This progression is mirrored in foreign trade and investment linkages. To stay ahead, the countries which developed first have been forced to move up the trade hierarchy and export more sophisticated products where they now have a comparative advantage, and FDI has provided a powerful tool for recycling comparative advantage through the transfer of technology and skills. This idea of a regional division of labour, combining an industrial and locational hierarchy has been described as a 'flying geese' development paradigm.[19]

Japan's role in this regional dynamic is complex. It has had a profound impact on the East Asian region as a model, and has demonstrated that spectacular results may be achieved through the right combination of state intervention and business enterprise. However, Japan's direct contribution to regional growth is more difficult to assess. The early evolution of its trade and FDI patterns do not provide a clear illustration of the kinds of linkages needed to generate a flying geese pattern of development. Although Japanese exports to the first-tier NIEs have mushroomed, it has not been a reciprocal market for their manufactured exports, and the Japanese market remains of secondary importance. Perhaps more significantly, until quite recently Japanese FDI in the region has been modest, particularly in manufacturing activities.

Japan's first wave of regional FDI began in the early 1970s, albeit one constrained by capital controls, adjustments to the oil shock and an undervalued yen, and by the late 1970s it was the leading investor in the region. However, much of this was in the primary sector, and even those strategic industries in the first-tier NIEs which relied more heavily on FDI did not rely on Japanese TNCs to any greater extent than firms from other advanced regions. Of course, this situation was, in part, a reflection of the strategic policy decisions of governments in these countries. Moreover, Japan did, in this context, play a quite significant role in transferring technology and strengthening management skills through various forms of technological agreements in certain industries.

The regional role of Japan has changed since the mid-1980s. The strong appreciation of the yen, emergence of new competitors in labour-intensive manufactures, protectionist pressures in the other major industrial countries and domestic macroeconomic pressures have led to a significant increase in Japanese FDI in the region: a first wave going to the first-tier NIEs after the yen appreciation in 1985, followed by a new wave in the early 1990s to the second-tier NIEs and, in particular, to China [*Akyüz, 1997*]. Large Japanese electronics and automobile producers have been especially prominent in these waves, often accompanied by smaller component suppliers. Moreover, because this recent wave of FDI has been accompanied by a significant rise in exports to Japan from the region, it appears to conform more closely to the relocation of manufacturing activities suggested by the flying geese pattern.

But despite this growing presence of Japan in the region, trade and FDI linkages appear to be stronger between the first- and second-tier NIEs. Trade between these countries is growing much faster than trade with the outside, and there has been a mushrooming of FDI from the first- to the second-tier NIEs. Together the first-tier NIEs represent a more important source of markets for other producers in the region than does Japan, and between them the first-tier NIEs now have more direct investment in South-East Asia than in Japan (Tables 4 and 5).

Although the expanding role of regional FDI has been an important feature of East Asian economic development over the past decade, its contribution to the growth process has not been spontaneous. Government policy has been central to the regional impact of FDI in determining both outward as well as inward FDI. It should not be forgotten that much of the international spillovers within East Asia have been ultimately generated because of the success of the industrial policy attempts of the North-East Asian economies, rather than through a purely market-generated process. Conversely, the effective use of FDI in facilitating industrial upgrading and technological catching-up has depended on a series of policy initiatives on the part of host governments.

TABLE 4
COMPOSITION OF THE STOCK OF FOREIGN DIRECT INVESTMENT
IN CHINA AND ASEAN-4 IN 1992, BY ORIGIN[a]
(Percentage)

| Origin | Total | ASEAN-4[b] | | | China[c] |
		Indonesia	Malaysia	Thailand	
Hong Kong	–	7.4	3.0	6.6	62.0 [d]
Republic of Korea	–	5.7	2.9	1.5	0.9
Singapore	–	4.1	6.7	6.3	–
Taiwan Province of China	–	7.7	22.8	9.2	8.2
Total first-tier NIEs	*25.8*	*24.9*	*35.4*	*23.6*	*71.1* [e]
Japan	26.1	15.7	22.7	38.1	8.4
United States	9.5	6.5	7.0	11.9	8.5
Other countries	38.6	52.9	35.0	26.4	12.0 [f]

Source: Ministry of International Trade and Industry, *White Paper on International Trade 1994*, Tokyo, 1994.
Notes: a Share of home countries listed in rows in total FDI stock in host countries listed in columns.
   b Indonesia, Malaysia, Thailand and the Philippines.
   c 1993.
   d Including also FDI from Macau.
   e Excluding FDI from Singapore, for which no separate data were available.
   f Including FDI from Singapore.

Moreover, some important features are already visible in the region that should caution against any simple projections of a regional integration process. The asymmetries in Japan's trade and FDI flows, even with its most advanced neighbours, have not only introduced serious regional imbalances, but the most recent upsurge of Japanese FDI to the region points to serious domestic imbalances, whose resolution will have an important bearing on Japan's wider regional role. Moreover, there is a growing incongruity between FDI seeking out cheap labour sources and the existing endowments of the South-East Asian economies facing acute labour shortages [*Jomo et al., 1997*]. In addition, there is considerable uncertainty surrounding the regional role of China, although its sheer size means that its integration with the rest of the region will be asymmetrical. The manner in which all these problems are resolved will have a major bearing on the future path of regional integration.

TABLE 5
EXPORTS OF MANUFACTURES FROM SELECTED EAST ASIAN COUNTRIES, BY
MAJOR DESTINATION, 1985 AND 1994
(Billions of dollars)

| Exports from | Developing East Asia | | | | | | | | | |
| | Total | | First-tier NIEs | | ASEAN-4 | | China | | Japan | |
To	1985	1994	1985	1994	1985	1994	1985	1994	1985	1994
World	102.2	483.8	82.7	281.7	10.2	102.5	9.3	99.6	169.4	377.8
Developing East Asia	19.1	173.2	13.1	101.9	2.9	34.3	3.1	37.0	39.7	142.3
First-tier NIEs	11.9	114.8	6.6	51.9	2.4	28.4	2.9	34.5	20.9	86.0
ASEAN-4	5.1	42.9	4.5	36.2	0.4	4.2	0.2	2.5	6.9	38.8
China	2.0	15.5	1.9	13.8	0.1	1.7	–	–	11.9	17.5
Japan	7.8	50.3	5.9	23.9	0.8	11.7	1.1	14.7	–	–
Other developed market economies	61.7	105.8	53.1	122.0	5.7	46.3	2.9	37.5	100.5	196.4
Rest of world	13.5	54.5	10.5	33.9	0.8	10.2	2.2	10.4	29.2	39.1

Source: UNCTAD data base.

III. LESSONS FOR OTHER DEVELOPING COUNTRIES

(1) Some General Remarks on the Question of Replicability

What are the lessons that other developing countries can draw from the experience of East Asian development? While this study has given considerable weight to institutional reform in explaining East Asian success, there is currently a widespread belief that many developing countries, especially in sub-Saharan Africa, lack the basic institutional infrastructure to manage complex economic policies, and therefore that the institutionally demanding policies used in East Asia have little relevance for them. There can be little doubt that in many developing countries years of civil strife or external conflict make the restoration of peace and basic social order an absolute prerequisite for any economic development. In other cases, the general economic crisis of the 1980s, the accompanying fiscal crisis of the state as well as the ideological shift against public activities have seriously weakened governments in every sense of the word, thus making it difficult to recommend very complex policies. But this does not mean that these countries should not consider longer-term development strategies. Indeed, the implication is rather that these strategies must be tied to wider efforts at rebuilding and reforming the institutions of the state and civil society [*van Arkadie, 1995*]. Ignoring certain elements on the grounds that countries presently lack the knowledge and capabilities to run them is likely to foreclose their evolution, and thereby frustrate future development strategies and policy choices.

However, an economic system is not something governments can change at will, but is a highly complex structure combining an array of legal, market and financial relations, formal and informal rules, shared values and traditional modes of behaviour, all of which are rooted in a country's social and political institutions. Moreover, these institutions comprise individuals and groups whose capabilities and knowledge are integral to the success of the institution to which they belong. Recognising this should lead policy-makers to expect the pace of institutional change to show considerable variation; radical changes in some areas will coexist with gradual evolution or even no change elsewhere. It is also true that there is no single mix of institutions that will work everywhere, given the differences in the economic, political, social and cultural profiles of individual countries. However – just as in the case of technology – being a late-comer and thus able to imitate institutional innovations made abroad can be an advantage.

As the contributions by Haggard *et al.* and Evans in this volume show, East Asian experience can be instructive. In a number of East Asian countries, not only did their development strategy evolve out of a period of deep economic and political crisis, but their bureaucracies on the eve of industrialisation were seen as just as inefficient as others in some of today's developing countries. Moreover, these same bureaucracies were often accused, by outside observers, of harbouring conservative practices and lacking the competence to organise their economic development. It is instructive to recall that until the 1960s, for example, Korea sent its bureaucrats to Pakistan for training in economic policy-making and, as noted above, in both Korea and Taiwan government–business relations were initially distant and at times quite tense.

Moreover, it is also comforting for developing countries to recognise that there are different ways to build institutions in support of long-term development goals. Korea's more interventionist policies were aimed, in part, at building strong business organisations, and relied heavily on close peak-level consultations between business leaders and government. By contrast, the state–business relationship in Taiwan, particularly in its formative years, was more distant and fragmented. None the less, in these and other cases in East Asia, it was only through persistent efforts at organisational reforms in areas of recruitment, promotion, compensation and training that these bureaucracies were improved. Much the same may be said of other institutions, such as the industry association, semi-public trading agencies and various public research institutes.

The success of East Asia can, in part, be linked to special conditions that are unlikely to be repeated elsewhere. However, the special-conditions argument is often presented in a very one-sided manner. For example, cold war politics may have provided large American aid flows to Korea and Taiwan, but it also imposed costs in the form of a greater defence burden, compulsory military service that reduced the available workforce, and, in the case of Korea, war devastation which cost millions of lives and destroyed well over 50 per cent of manufacturing capacity and infrastructure. To take another example, the frequently heard reference to the beneficial effect of Confucianism through its emphasis on education, social discipline and good government contrasts with previous descriptions of a culture stifling individual initiative and encouraging 'irrational' preference for bureaucratic, rather than business or engineering, careers.

The important point is not whether a particular set of initial economic and cultural conditions helps to equip a society better for economic development than another, as all such conditions contain elements which may either hold back or support future development, but to explore whether and how the pro-developmental elements can best be promoted. However, because the question of initial conditions involves not only domestic circumstances but the wider international context, particular attention needs to be given to changes in the world economy and whether the kinds of policies identified with East Asia's development institutions can still be pursued, even if they are potentially beneficial to growth and industrialisation, and even assuming countries have the domestic capacity to implement them.

(2) Institutional Capability-Building

Where might the initial steps of institutional reform begin in developing countries? In East Asia the best results during their initial period of growth were achieved when governments were pursuing a limited number of selective interventions in certain strategic import-substitution and export-oriented industries, which contributed to the accumulation of capabilities and know-how that proved extremely useful in conducting more sophisticated interventionist policies used for promoting the next generation of industries. In the first-tier NIEs these policies were targeted at low-skill manufactured industries. The lessons from South-East Asia suggest that similar measures can be applied to improving agriculture and resource extraction, and that designing policies to attract FDI and maximise the gains from hosting TNCs in selective areas may provide a particularly important area for policy-makers in this first stage of industrial development. Thus, engagement in a limited number of complex policies during the initial stages of export promotion will allow the government to learn how to design sectoral policies, find out what incentives are effective for what purpose, and to learn about the loopholes that a policy that looks good on paper may have, and so on.

One factor that appears crucial in this process concerns the organisation of the civil service. This involves a number of features. First of all, the core of the bureaucracy needs to be given a substantial degree of insulation from political pressures. Although total insulation is neither possible nor desirable (as this can make the bureaucracy unresponsive to an important source of change), if the bureaucracy is unduly subject to the pressures of day-to-day politics, it will be less able to devise and modify policies in the light of its own experience, and is more likely to become overburdened with multiple objectives, many of which will be short-term in nature. In all the East Asian countries, the need to make bold policy changes, whether in response to external shocks or switches to more export-oriented strategies, have undoubtedly been helped by the autonomy of their economic bureaucracies.

A second feature involves the degree of personnel continuity in the civil service. Only part of the technology of policy-making can be embodied in organisational structure and rules. Much will depend upon the accumulated knowledge of civil servants, and it is necessary to find ways to maximise the application of their tacit knowledge. One thing that characterised the East Asian bureaucracy, following their reform in the 1950s and the 1960s, was the continuity of its personnel, if not necessarily the organisational structure.

Thirdly, while insulating the bureaucracy from day-to-day pressures and preserving personnel continuity may be necessary for the accumulation of policy experiences, this will not be adequately digested if the quality of the personnel is low. Both Korea and Taiwan – and before them Japan – introduced from an early date a strict meritocracy into the bureaucracy. Both countries have encouraged strong organisational goals and loyalties by recruiting from top educational establishments, promoting from within and providing attractive remuneration packages. While there may be more than one way to incorporate talented people into the civil service, it is absolutely necessary that the core bureaucrats have high learning capabilities if policies are to be improved over time.[20]

The competence of the bureaucracy is only part of the institutional context required to design and implement an effective development strategy. Such strategies are even more effective if accompanied by a good working relationship between the bureaucracy and the private sector, because this will allow the bureaucracy to acquire more detailed information concerning the capabilities and shortcomings of the private sector. Peak organisations representing business have played an important role in mediating relations between industry and the state in a number of East Asian economies, although they have evolved slowly.

However, the details of policy design and implementation are not the sole responsibility of 'big' institutions, but have often been embedded in a denser network of institutional relations between the government and private sector. Indeed, the core efforts of institutional design in East Asia appear to have been through formal and informal ties created at the sectoral level. These agencies have embodied high levels of professionalism and competence, and have been better placed to establish close working relations with their private-sector counterparts. In particular, as countries have shifted to more complex industrial activities, these institutions have played an important role in overcoming problems of incomplete, imperfect or asymmetric information. Sector-specific agencies have often taken a lead role in promoting new investment opportunities, forging links with foreign suppliers and investors, and facilitating technological upgrading. Consultative councils, and other forms of government–business links, have also played an important role in enhancing the transparency and fairness of administrative decision-making, forcing decision-makers to clarify and justify their actions, facilitating information flows, and providing a forum for solving conflicts and coordination problems that characterise economic policies.

(3) Responding to the New Global Environment

The East Asian experience shows that an active and fruitful participation in the global economy requires a deliberate approach to international integration through a measured and properly sequenced set of policies towards trade, capital flows and FDI. The first-tier NIEs opened up different sectors of their economies to foreign competition in different degrees according to their national policy objectives: relatively open in trade, except in 'strategic' industries and luxury consumption goods; more restrictive on technology licensing; much more restrictive on FDI, except in certain export-oriented, labour-intensive industries; extremely restrictive on capital flows, until their economies attained relatively high levels of development; and so on. The second-tier NIEs have deviated from this pattern in certain areas, in part because their starting points were different. The differing degrees of openness in different areas were not simply an accident, but determined by their long-term industrial strategy, which, as discussed earlier, put emphasis on channelling the available surplus into productive investments, supported by attempts to develop domestic technological capabilities. Thus, the East Asian countries have shown that a selective, strategic approach to the liberalisation of trade and investment remains a key to success in the global economy.

However, there is a perception that emulation by developing countries of the selective strategies followed by the successful East Asian NIEs may no longer be possible. First, because the kind of export dynamism available to the East Asian NIEs has been significantly diminished as more and more countries pursue an export-oriented strategy. Secondly, because the intensification of multilateral trade disciplines and the extension of their scope as a result of the Uruguay Round prohibits the use of some key policy tools, such as export subsidies and infant industry protection, central to the export success of these countries. In response to this dilemma, it is increasingly argued that the only viable option may be to actively and fully integrate into the global economy, rather than pursue a more selective strategy along East Asian lines.

Regarding the danger of a 'fallacy of composition' in manufactured exports, while there is some evidence that this could become a constraint on industrial development in the South, particularly if slow growth persists in the advanced industrial countries, the potential scope for developing countries to enter Northern markets for textiles, clothing and other such goods is considerable [*UNCTAD, 1996*]. Moreover, the very success of the East Asian economies means not only that they are facing pressures to vacate these markets and shift to higher value-added exports, but also that their own markets for low-skill manufactures are expanding, providing new export opportunities for the next generation of industrialising countries.

It is the case that the new trading regime under the WTO has reduced the scope for using measures such as trade-related subsidies, lax enforcement of intellectual property rights, and strategic conditions imposed on foreign investments, which were integral parts of the East Asian development strategy [*Das, 1997*]. Certainly, the more generalised protection which provided a backdrop for targeted policies in East Asia is no longer possible. It may also be true that the changes will reduce the scope for policy manoeuvre for developing countries wishing to pursue a strategy involving vigorous infant industry protection and export subsidies. This appears to be particularly the case with the trade related investment measures (TRIMs) and intellectual property (TRIPs) agreements [*Singh, 1996*].

However, when assessing the design of appropriate policies under current international obligations, it should be recalled that the East Asian countries had to exercise a considerable amount of policy ingenuity and administrative and diplomatic skills to maintain some of their policies.[21] Moreover, although the Uruguay Round has clearly increased disciplines, it has also improved security of market access for exports from developing countries. This represents an improvement over the conditions faced by many East Asian NIEs.[22] It is equally the case that the policy-making process operates quite differently where a large part of economic activity is organised through internal markets and close firm-level contacts, as was the case in a number of the first-tier NIEs. In other words, the basic argument which must be addressed is not whether the loss to developing countries in terms of policy autonomy is fully compensated by gains in terms of market access. It is rather whether, in light of changes in the global environment, there still remains a need for new policies to strengthen the prospects of developing countries and whether the East Asian experience remains a relevant source for such policies in today's trading system.

With respect to *infant industry protection*, it should be noted that none of the East Asian NIEs ever had resort to the 'infant industry' clause of GATT, but quantitative restrictions were covered under the developing country balance-of-payments provisions. This possibility remains open to developing countries meeting the balance-of-payments criteria, although the 'Understanding' relating to this Article strongly discourages resort to quantitative measures and provides for stricter multilateral surveillance. However, to the extent that tariff rates remain unbound or bound at ceiling levels above currently applied rates, they can be increased to protect 'infant industries'.

The Agreement on Subsidies and Countervailing Measures defines 'subsidy' for the first time, tightens the disciplines on subsidies, and extends these disciplines to all WTO members. However, it is perhaps this Agreement which contains the most meaningful provisions on differential and more favourable treatment for poorer countries, some of which are not subject to any precise time limits. For example, the least developed countries and a list of 20 other countries with GDP per capita of less than $1,000 are exempt from the prohibition of export subsidies so long as they remain in these categories and certain thresholds, based on shares of world markets for products benefiting from export subsidies, are not reached. Other developing countries are subject to an eight-year phase-out of prohibited subsidies. Although 'specific' subsidies (that is, those limited to certain enterprises and not granted according to neutral, objective criteria) are 'actionable', 'remedies' may be applied against 'actionable' subsidies of developing countries only if injury to the domestic industry of another member, serious prejudice to its interests or nullification of concessions can be demonstrated. In addition, there are a set of non-actionable subsidies, including those which are intended to promote basic research, agriculture and regional development.

In summary, while the WTO multilateral agreements have reduced the scope of some policy options, strategies comparable to those used earlier by the East Asian countries can still be applied, particularly by the poorer countries. The main constraints would seem to be those imposed by the ability of the countries concerned to devise and execute such policies, particularly those involving negotiations with developed countries or TNCs, and to do this in the time periods available which differ among countries and from one Agreement to the other. In this context, both formal and informal government–business links which played such an important role in East Asia's success are likely to be of growing importance in the new trading environment, and measures to strengthen government–industry partnerships deserve closer attention by developing countries.

More importantly, it should be noted that there are many policy measures that remain outside the scope of WTO obligations. Government provision of information to exporters and changes to exchange rates remain permissible policy instruments. Policies may be designed in such a way that they serve both macroeconomic purposes and others, such as increasing the international competitiveness of certain industries. Many of the policies identified earlier with a dynamic profit–investment nexus can still be so designed as to be permissible under the new trading rules (see the contribution by Singh). These include general fiscal concessions to corporations, the provision of subsidised R&D, measures to promote corporate savings and investment, and differential taxes (VAT and excise tax) on domestic consumption and production. Given that these policies can have considerable influence on promoting technological upgrading and international competitiveness, strengthening these areas of policy-making cannot be emphasised too strongly.

IV. CONCLUSIONS

The East Asian developmental experience offers some very interesting lessons on how poor economies dependent on natural resources can make an effective transition to labour-intensive manufacturing, and then to more complex manufacturing industries essential for the attainment of high standards of living. It shows how important it is to channel resources into those groups, including business corporations, which have the capacity to make investments, to ensure that these investments are made in the right areas and to monitor whether they are managed in such a way as to increase long-term productivity.

In the earlier stages of industrial transition, identifying the right areas for investment and ensuring their productivity growth may not require very selective policies, but when a country needs to move beyond the static comparative advantage industries, such policies become more necessary. As some critics rightly argue, these policies require a competent bureaucracy and institutions to facilitate co-operation between the government and the private sector, and therefore cannot be easily replicated in other countries which lack these conditions. But it should not be forgotten that these institutions can be constructed and improved through conscious efforts. In fact, their construction is one secret of East Asian success. The changing international trading environment may be restricting the freedom of developing countries to conduct East-Asian-style policies, but there is considerable scope for manoeuvre if countries skilfully use various 'permissible' subsidies, balance-of-payment clauses, non-trade-related policy measures, and are more creative in interpreting the new international trading rules.

It is clear that there is no single path to development which fits every country. However, recognising institutional diversity should not be confused with the argument that therefore there are no lessons to be learnt from the East Asian experience. It is both possible and instructive to identify some major principles that underlie this successful experience, and to try to adapt the policy tools and institutional vehicles that were used to realise those principles in order to fit local conditions elsewhere, and if necessary to devise new policy tools and institutions. Indeed, if East Asian governments had themselves believed in the impossibility of such institutional adaptation and innovation and had ignored earlier success stories, it is doubtful whether we would have an East Asian Miracle to discuss.

NOTES

1. Unless otherwise qualified, the designation East Asia will be used here to refer to the whole region, including Japan, the first-tier newly industrializing countries (NIEs – namely, the Republic of Korea, Taiwan Province of China, Hong Kong and Singapore), second-tier NIEs (Indonesia, Malaysia and Thailand), and the newly emerging market economies, as well as China.
2. For examples of this approach, see Balassa [1971], Fei and Ranis [1975], and Myint [1982].
3. See Magaziner and Hout [1980], Johnson [1982], Boltho [1985], and Dore [1986]. At the same time, Japanese scholars also began to offer their own perspective on post-war Japanese success, including criticism of conventional economic explanations [Shinohara, 1982; Komiya et al., 1988; Tsuru, 1993].
4. The seminal contributions were Amsden [1989] and Wade [1990].
5. See also Chowdhury and Islam [1993].
6. There have, of course, been important differences between these two island economies. In particular, Hong Kong's more laissez-faire policy stance has led to weak structural change within industry along with a rapid shift to services [UNCTAD, 1996].
7. The contributions by Haggard et al. and Singh in this volume consider these and other differences in greater detail.
8. In this respect, it should be noted at the outset that institutional adaptation and innovation in late-industrializing countries make it inevitable that different countries embarking on economic development at the same point in time end up with different institutions and policy mechanisms, even if they follow a broadly similar strategy; this was the case for the successful European industrialisers of the late 19th century, such as Germany, Sweden and

Switzerland. Thus, in principle there is no contradiction between acknowledging differences among the East Asian countries, or between North-East and South-East Asia, and the search for common principles in their experiences.

9. For an examination of the limits of conventional analysis in this respect, see Akyüz and Gore [1996].

10. For a recent statement of this position, see Sachs and Warner [1995]; World Bank [1996].

11. For a fuller discussion, see UNCTAD [1994]; Akyüz and Gore [1996], Rodrik [1995], and Tanzi and Shome [1992].

12. On the disciplining of investment in Korea, see Chang [1993]; on Taiwan, see Wade [1990: 256–96].

13. For a recent discussion, see Helleiner [1995].

14. There is indeed considerable evidence to show that the role of exports to finance imports is a significant one, albeit one that varies significantly over time owing to the availability of foreign exchange from other sources [Esfahani, 1991; Fung et al., 1994].

15. In the case of Taiwan resource-intensive manufactured exports remained relatively important as a source of foreign exchange for a longer period of time [Hentschel, 1992].

16. For a further discussion of the role of FDI in East Asia, see UNCTAD [1996], Rasiah [1995], Lall [1995a], Chang [1998] and Akyüz [1997].

17. For recent discussion on the second-tier NIEs, see Lall [1995a; 1995b], Rock [1995], Hill [1995], and Jomo et al. [1997].

18. These passages were drafted before the recent crisis in South-East Asia. See also UNCTAD [1996: 102, 123].

19. For a fuller account of the flying geese paradigm and regional dynamics in East Asia, see UNCTAD [1996: Part Two, Ch.I].

20. Korea attempted a much wider reform of the civil service and relied more on dedicated career bureaucrats, whereas Taiwan was more willing to identify special career tracks and recruit external people in mid-career. On bureaucrats learning from their mistakes in Korea, see Mytelka [forthcoming].

21. These constraints were different for each of the East Asian economies. For example, Japan became a contracting party to GATT in 1955 and Korea in 1967, Hong Kong applied the GATT as a separate customs territory of the United Kingdom, while Singapore applied the GATT de facto as of 1966 and became a contracting party by succession in 1973. On the other hand, Taiwan is only now seeking accession to the WTO (as the separate customs territory of 'Chinese Taipei'). Japan became a signatory to all the Tokyo Round Codes on non-tariff measures, while Korea, Hong Kong and Singapore accepted only some of them. Korea continued to apply restrictions under the balance-of-payments provisions and did not disinvoke Article XVIII.B until during the Uruguay Round.

22. However, most benefited from GSP treatment in the major markets, and in fact, were among the beneficiaries showing the highest rate of utilisation of GSP schemes. However, Japan faced discriminatory quantitative restrictions for many years after joining GATT, as many countries invoked the non-application clause against it. The other countries also faced a series of non-tariff barriers, including voluntary export restraints in textiles and clothing and other sectors, as well as the threat of countervailing duties applied without the 'injury test' by the United States (until the acceptance of the Tokyo Round Code).

REFERENCES

Akyüz, Y., 1993, 'Financial liberalisation: The Key Issues', in Y. Akyüz and G. Held (eds.), Finance and the Real Economy, Santiago: ECLAC.

Akyüz, Y., 1998, 'New Trends in Japanese Trade and FDI: Post-Industrial Transformation and Policy Challenge', in Kozul-Wright and Rowthorn [1998].

Akyüz, Y. and C. Gore, 1996, 'The Investment–Profits Nexus in East Asian Industrialisation', World Development, Vol.24, No.3.

Amsden, A., 1989, Asia's Next Giant: South Korea and Late Industrialisation, New York: Oxford University Press.

Amsden, A., 1991, 'Big Business and Urban Congestion in Taiwan: The Origins of Small Enterprise and Regionally Decentralised Industry", *World Development*, Vol.19, No.9.

Balassa, B., 1971, 'Industrial Policies in Taiwan and Korea', *Weltwirtschsftliches Archiv*, Vol.106, No.1.

Boltho, A., 1985, 'Was Japan's Industrial Policy Successful?', *Cambridge Journal of Economics*, Vol.9, No.2.

Chang, H.-J., 1993, 'The Political Economy of Industrial Policy in Korea', *Cambridge Journal of Economics*, Vol.17, No.2.

Chang, H.-J., 1994, *The Political Economy of Industrial Policy*, London: Macmillan.

Chang, H.-J., 1995, 'Transnational Corporations and Industrial Strategy', in Kozul-Wright and Rowthorn [*1998*].

Chowdhury, A. and I. Islam, 1993, *The Newly Industrializing Economies of East Asia*, London: Routledge.

Das, B.L., 1997, 'WTO Agreements: Defficiencies, Imbalances and Required Changes', *Third World Network Briefing Paper*, Oct., Geneva: UNCTAD.

De Long, B. and L. Summers, 1991, 'Equipment Investment and Economic Growth', *Quarterly Journal of Economics*, Vol.106, No.2.

Dore, R., 1986, *Flexible Rigidities: Industrial Policy and Structural Adjustment in the Japanese Economy 1970–1980*, London: The Athlone Press.

Esfahani, H.S., 1991, 'Exports, Imports and Economic Growth in Semi-Industrialised Countries, *Journal of Development Economics*, Vol.35.

Fei, J. and G. Ranis, 1975, 'A Model of Growth and Employment in the Open Dualistic Economy: The Cases of Korea and Taiwan', in F. Stewart (ed.), *Employment, Income Distribution and Development*, London: Frank Cass.

Field, K., 1995, *Enterprise and the State in Korea and Taiwan*, Ithaca, NY: Cornell University.

Fung, H.G., Sawhney, B., Lo, W.C. and P. Xiang, 1994, 'Exports, Imports and Industrial Production: Evidence from Advanced and Newly Industrializing Countries", *International Economic Journal*, Vol.8.

Helleiner, G., 1995, 'Trade, Trade Policy and Industrialisation Reconsidered', *World Development Studies*, No.6, Helsinki: UNU/WIDER.

Hentschel, J., 1992, 'Productivity Growth and Structural Change in Industry and Trade in Five South-East Asian Countries', UNCTAD, Technology Programme, Technological Dynamism Project, Geneva: United Nations.

Hill, H., 1995, 'Indonesia: From Chronic Dropout to Miracle?', *Journal of International Development*, Vol.7, No.5.

Hirschman, A., 1995, *A Propensity to Self-Subversion*, Cambridge, MA: Harvard University Press.

Johnson, C., 1982, *MITI and the Japanese Miracle*, Stanford, CA: Stanford University Press.

Jomo, K. *et al.*, 1997, *Southeast Asia's Misunderstood Miracle*, Boulder, CO: Westview Press.

Komiya, R., Okuno, O. and K. Suzumura, 1988, *Industrial Policy of Japan*, London: Academic Press.

Kozul-Wright, R. and B. Rowthorn (eds.), 1998, *Transnational Corporations in the Global Economy*, London: Macmillan.

Lall, S., 1995a, 'Industrial Strategy and Policies on Foreign Direct Investment in East Asia', *Transnational Corporations*, Vol.4, No.3.

Lall, S., 1995b, 'Malaysia: Industrial Success and the Role of Government', *Journal of International Development*, Vol.7, No.5.

Magaziner, I. and T. Hout, 1980, *Japanese Industrial Policy*, London: Policy Studies Institute.

Myint, H., 1982, 'Comparative Analysis of Taiwan's Economic Development with Other Countries', in *Experiences and Lessons of Economic Development in Taiwan*, Taipei: Institute of Economics, Academia Sinica.

Mytelka, L., forthcoming, 'Learning, Innovation, and Industrial Policy: Some Lessons from Korea', in M. Storper *et al.* (eds.), *Industrial Policies for Latecomers*, London: Routledge.

Rasiah, R., 1995, *Foreign Capital and Industrialisation in Malaysia*, London: Macmillan.

Rock, M., 1995, 'Thai Industrial Policy: How Irrelevant Was It?', *Journal of International Development*, Vol.7, No.5.

Rodrik, D., 1995, 'Getting Intervention Right: How South Korea and Taiwan Grew Rich',
    Economic Policy, No.20.
Sachs, J. and A. Warner, 1995, 'Economic Reform and the Process of Global Integration',
    Brookings Papers on Economic Activity, No.1.
Schmidt-Hebbel, K., Serven, L. and A. Solimano, 1996, 'Savings and Investment: Paradigms,
    Puzzles, Policies', *The World Bank Research Observer*, Vol.11, No.1.
Shinohara, M., 1982, *Industrial Growth, Trade and Dynamic Patterns in the Japanese Economy*,
    Tokyo: University of Tokyo Press.
Singh, A., 1995, 'The Causes of Fast Economic Growth in East Asia', *UNCTAD Review*, New
    York and Geneva: United Nations.
Singh, A., 1996, 'The Post-Uruguay Round World Trading System, Industrialisation, Trade and
    Development: Implications for the Asia-Pacific Developing Countries', in *Expansion of
    Trading Opportunities to the Year 2000 for Asia-Pacific Developing Countries: Implications
    of the Uruguay Round and Adaptation of Export Strategies*, Geneva: UNCTAD.
Stiglitz, J., 1994, 'The Role of the State in Financial Markets', *Proceedings of the World Bank
    Conference on Development Economics 1993*, Washington, DC: World Bank.
Stiglitz, J. and M. Uy, 1996, 'Financial Markets, Public Policy and the East Asian Miracle', *The
    World Bank Research Observer*, Vol.11, No.2.
Studart, R., 1995, *Investment Finance in Economic Development*, London: Routledge.
Tanzi, V. and P. Shome, 1992, 'The Role of Taxation in the Development of East Asian
    Economies', in T. Oto and A.O. Krueger (eds.), *The Political Economy of Tax Reform*,
    Chicago, IL: Chicago University Press.
Tsuru, S., 1993, *Japan's Capitalism: Creative Defeat and Beyond*, Cambridge: Cambridge
    University Press.
UNCTAD, 1992, *Trade and Development Report, 1992*, New York and Geneva: United Nations.
UNCTAD, 1994, *Trade and Development Report, 1994*, New York and Geneva: United Nations.
UNCTAD, 1996, *Trade and Development Report, 1996*, New York and Geneva: United Nations.
UNCTAD, 1997, *Trade and Development Report, 1997*, New York and Geneva: United Nations.
van Arkadie, B., 1995, 'The State and Economic Change in Africa', in H.-J. Chang and R.
    Rowthorn (eds.), *The Role of the State in Economic Change*, Oxford: Clarendon Press.
Wade, R., 1990, *Governing the Market: Economic Theory and the Role of Government in East
    Asian Industrialisation*, Princeton, NJ: Princeton University Press.
World Bank, 1993, *The East Asian Miracle: Economic Growth and Public Policy*, Oxford:
    Oxford University Press.
World Bank, 1996, *Global Economic Prospects and the Developing Countries*, Washington, DC:
    World Bank.

Income Distribution and Growth in East Asia

JONG-IL YOU

It is widely believed that the East Asian economies performed exceptionally well not only in generating growth but also in keeping inequality low. This study tries to answer the questions raised by the claims of exceptionality of income distribution in East Asia. Central findings are that only Japan, Korea and Taiwan have legitimate claims to low inequality; that the East Asian economies distinguished themselves by their ability to translate high profit shares into high savings and investment rates; and that low inequality and high profit shares coexisted primarily due to the unusually even distribution of wealth.

Europe was so organised socially and economically as to secure the maximum accumulation of capital. While there was some continuous improvement in the daily condition of the mass of the population, society was so framed as to throw a great part of the increased income into the control of the class least likely to consume it ... Herein lay in fact the main justification of the capitalist system. If the rich had spent their new wealth on their own enjoyment, the world would long ago have found such a regime intolerable [*Keynes, 1919: 18*].

INTRODUCTION

Faster growth and more egalitarian income distribution have been the main objectives of development. There is a wide-ranging consensus among economists that East Asia holds a special place in the developing world as a case in which both these objectives have been successfully attained. *The*

Jong-Il You, KDI School of International Policy and Management. The initial version of this study was prepared as a background paper for the UNCTAD *Trade and Development Report 1997*. The author wishes to thank Ha-Joon Chang, Lance Taylor, Yilmaz Akyüz and the editors of *The Journal of Development Studies* for their useful comments.

East Asian Miracle report by the World Bank [*1993*] (to be referred to henceforth as *The Miracle* report) mirrors this consensus in its analysis of the economic success of what it calls the High Performing Asian Economies (HPAEs) – Japan, the Republic of Korea (simply Korea hereafter), Taiwan, Hong Kong, Singapore, Malaysia, Thailand and Indonesia. It says that the essence of the miracle is the rapid growth combined with 'unusually low and declining income inequality, underscoring the exceptional nature of this achievement'.

If this is correct, the contrast with the historical experience of the European development as analysed by Kuznets or described in the above quote from Keynes could not be stronger. The first contrast is about whether growth tends to increase or decrease inequality. Another difference is whether greater or less inequality is conducive to growth. Yet another difference concerns the political economy of distribution and growth: does growth lead people to accept inequality or does a good distribution lead people to accept growth-oriented policies? Is the East Asian experience truly exceptional? Do we now have to discard the classical/Keynesian understanding of the accumulation process based on profits?

The interaction between policies, income distribution and growth is complex. This study tries to sort out some of the issues and answer the questions raised by the claims of exceptionality of income distribution in East Asia. The central findings are (i) that the exceptionality claim has a limited validity with respect to Japan, Korea and Taiwan only, where low inequality prevails as a consequence of the exceptionally equal initial distribution of wealth resulting from post-war reforms and the rapid employment expansion in the subsequent growth process; (ii) that the classical/Keynesian view of the accumulation process, in which high profits play a crucial role as a source of savings and an incentive for investment, is very much relevant in understanding the East Asian experience; (iii) that a relatively high inequality in the functional distribution of income went hand in hand with a relatively low inequality in the size distribution, primarily owing to the unusually even distribution of wealth, resulting from the initial conditions as well as the rather high savings propensity of the low-income households.

The rest of the study is devoted to substantiating the above claims and organised as follows. We begin by an examination of the records and explanation of income distribution in East Asia (section I). In the next section, we analyse the relationship between income distribution and the accumulation process in East Asia from the classical/Keynesian perspective (section II). Then, we go on to discuss the reasons why East Asian countries managed to have low inequality despite relatively high shares of profits in income (section III). The following section presents an analytical framework on the relationship between growth and income distribution within which the East Asian experience can be understood (section IV). The concluding section V provides a brief summary.

I. IS EAST ASIAN INCOME DISTRIBUTION TRULY EXCEPTIONAL?

(1) Level of Inequality: Not All in the Same League

Here we examine the evidence on income inequality in East Asia to see if they are truly exceptional. An appropriate place to start the discussion is *The Miracle* report. The World Bank economists classify only seven economies as 'high growth-low inequality' in a sample of 40, all of which are HPAEs, with Malaysia as the only HPAE that does not qualify [*World Bank, 1993: Fig. 1.3: 31*]. Putting aside the question of reliability of the data, this impressive evidence of 'growth with equity' in East Asia becomes suspect once we ask what the rationale for sample selection is. *The Miracle* report gives absolutely no explanation whatsoever. We do not know why France, Switzerland and Spain are included in the sample, but Germany, Sweden and Portugal are not; nor do we have a clue as to why India, Colombia and Mauritius are, but China, Costa Rica and Morocco are not. It seems therefore worthwhile to see if the conclusion of *The Miracle* report stands when we change the reference samples.

For obvious reasons, we shall use the World Bank's own data [*World Bank, 1994: Table 30*] and the inequality measure it uses (the ratio of the income shares of the richest 20 per cent and the poorest 20 per cent of the population).[1] As a way of excluding arbitrariness from the sample choice, we may consider a sample that includes all countries for which the data are available from the above World Bank table. To this, we add Taiwan to get a more complete picture on the HPAEs, using the official government data for 1990 taken from CEPD [*1995*]. This gives us a sample of 66 economies, and Table 1 ranks them from the lowest inequality to the highest. It shows that Japan, Indonesia, Taiwan and Korea may indeed be characterised as having low income inequalities as they rank in the top third of the sample. The other four HPAEs, however, rank in the bottom half, with Malaysia ranking in the bottom third. Given this, it seems unreasonable to say that the HPAEs as a group stand out for their low inequalities. Excluding from the sample the outliers – the three former socialist countries at the top of the ranking and the seven poor countries with the inequality ratio over 20 – hardly changes the overall picture.

Next, we consider dividing the sample into groups according to the growth performance. From the reduced sample of 56 economies that excludes the outliers, we construct a high-growth group (12 economies), a

TABLE 1

RANKING OF INCOME INEQUALITY IN 66 COUNTRIES

Country	IR	Rank	Country	IR	Rank	Country	IR	Rank
Hungary	3.2	1	Finland	6.0	23	Australia	9.6	45
Bulgaria	3.5	2	Italy	6.0	24	UK	9.6	46
Poland	3.9	3	Ghana	6.3	25	Venezuela	10.3	47
Rwanda	4.0	4	China	6.5	26	Peru	10.5	48
Bangladesh	4.1	5	Israel	6.6	27	*Malaysia*	11.7	49
Japan	4.3	6	Algeria	6.7	28	Costa Rica	12.7	50
Nepal	4.3	7	Morocco	7.0	29	Mauritania	13.2	51
Spain	4.4	8	Canada	7.1	30	Dominican R.	13.2	52
Sri Lanka	4.4	9	Denmark	7.1	31	Mexico	13.6	53
Netherlands	4.5	10	Jordan	7.3	32	Colombia	15.5	54
Belgium	4.6	11	Philippines	7.4	33	Zimbabwe	15.6	55
Sweden	4.6	12	France	7.5	34	Botswana	16.4	56
India	4.7	13	Tunisia	7.8	35	Senegal	16.7	57
Pakistan	4.7	14	Jamaica	8.1	36	Chile	17.0	58
Ethiopia	4.8	15	*Thailand*	8.3	37	Kenya	18.2	59
Indonesia	4.9	16	Switzerland	8.6	38	Lesotho	20.7	60
Uganda	4.9	17	Bolivia	8.6	39	Honduras	23.5	61
Taiwan	5.2	18	*Hong Kong*	8.7	40	Tanzania	26.1	62
Korea	5.7	19	New Zealand	8.8	41	Guinea-Bissau	28.0	63
Germany	5.8	20	Zambia	8.9	42	Panama	29.9	64
Côte d'Ivoire	5.8	21	USA	8.9	43	Guatemala	30.0	65
Norway	5.9	22	*Singapore*	9.6	44	Brazil	32.1	66

Source: Calculated from *World Development Report, 1994*, Table 30.

Note: IR (inequality ratio) = income share of the top quantile/income share of the bottom quantile.

medium-growth group (22 economies) and a low-growth group (22 economies).[2] Figure 1 depicts the median and the average inequality ratios of each of the three groups as well as the inequality ratios of all the HPAEs. An interesting feature of this figure is the negative relationship between growth and median inequality, which suggests a possibility that countries with lower inequality have better chances of high economic growth. As for the HPAEs, all of them except Japan belong to the high-growth group. Among them, only three (Indonesia, Taiwan, Korea) have lower inequality than the group median, and the other four have higher inequality than both the group average and the group median. Neither the most equal countries (Nepal, India, Pakistan) nor the most unequal country (Botswana) in this group are HPAEs. This finding flies in the face of *The Miracle* report's claim that all the high growth-low inequality countries are HPAEs.

Finally, we consider the inequality rankings within groups of economies classified on the basis of the level of income. This is probably the most significant exercise, given that the level of income is thought to be one of

FIGURE 1

INEQUALITY ACROSS GROWTH GROUPS AND IN HPAEs

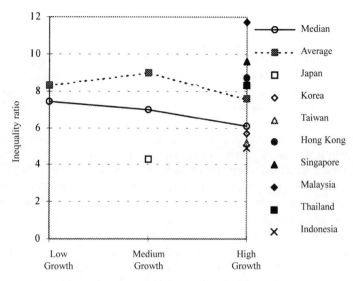

Source: Calculated from Table 1 above and World Bank [*1994*: *Table 2*].

FIGURE 2

INEQUALITY ACROSS INCOME GROUPS AND IN HPAEs

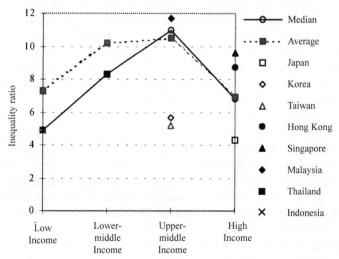

Source: Calculated from Table 1 above.

the basic determinants of inequality. We follow the World Bank classification of countries into four levels of income and obtain a low income group (15 economies), a lower-middle income group (15 economies), an upper-middle income group (six economies), and a high income group (20 economies). Figure 2, which depicts the median and the average inequality ratios of each of these four groups, clearly supports the Kuznets hypothesis of an inverted U-shaped relationship between inequality and the level of income. Both the median and the average inequality rise as the level of income rises up to the upper-middle income, before falling at the high income level.

From Figure 2 we can also compare the inequality ratios of the HPAEs with the average and the median of the income groups to which they belong. Among the three HPAEs that belong to the high income group, only Japan has low inequality. Inequality in Hong Kong and Singapore is at the higher end of this group. In the upper-middle income group Taiwan and Korea have low inequality, but Malaysia's inequality is very high. Among the lower-middle income economies, Thailand is the only HPAE and its inequality is the same as the group median (though lower than the group average). As the only HPAE that belongs to the low income group, Indonesia's inequality is also the same as the median of this group.

It is clearly an overstatement to say that the HPAEs all have 'unusually low inequality'. Instead, in terms of inequality, we have three sub-groups within the HPAEs: Japan, Korea and Taiwan – let us call them 'the super three' – indeed deserve to be thus described. Thailand and Indonesia have the median inequality in their respective income groups; while Malaysia, Hong Kong and Singapore have one of the highest inequality in their respective income groups.[3] The diversity of HPAEs in terms of income inequality in comparison to other countries in their income group is not surprising, once we recognise that the model of development itself is diverse within the HPAEs [*Perkins, 1994*].

(2) Declining Income Inequality: More than Meets the Eye

Based on a comparison of the average growth rates and the changes in the Gini coefficient from the 1960s to the 1980s in 15 developing countries [*World Bank, 1993: Fig. 1.1: 4*], *The Miracle* report claims that in the HPAEs, except for Korea and Taiwan, income distribution improved by as much as, or more than, in other developing economies. Furthermore, it notes the uniqueness of the HPAEs in combining high growth and declining inequality. Both these claims seem stretched.

First, there is a question about the sample choice. In particular, it is nonsensical to say that the HPAEs are unique in combining high growth and declining inequality in a sample that does not contain any other high-growth countries. If the implicit reference group were the advanced Western countries that followed the inverted-U curve of Kuznets, it would not be a valid comparison, since their historical growth rates were not as high as those of today's high-growth developing countries.

Second, even in the given sample, declining inequality is nothing unique to East Asia, nor is the East Asian performance in this regard particularly distinguished. *The seven developing HPAEs rank second, third, fifth, seventh, eighth, eleventh and twelfth out of the 15 samples.* To say that Korea and Taiwan are exceptions because they began with highly equal income distribution is rather deceptive, unless some reason is given why it becomes more difficult to reduce inequality if initial inequality is low. In fact, as we see below, these countries had large reductions in inequality from their low initial level at the early stages of high growth, and it is because of the recent rise in inequality that the reductions during the three decades 1960s–80s turn out to be small.

If we look at the more detailed picture on the change in inequality in the HPAEs, the rosy picture put out by the World Bank is substantially undermined. Figure 3 shows the time path of inequality as measured by the Gini coefficient in the HPAEs minus Indonesia from late 1950s to mid-1980s. The performance of the HPAEs in reducing inequality as seen in Figure 3 is not unequivocally good. Both Malaysia and Thailand show higher levels of inequality at the end of the period than at the beginning. Furthermore, with Korea, Malaysia and Thailand showing something like the inverted-U curve pattern and Taiwan, Hong Kong and Singapore showing the opposite trend of U-shaped curves, while Japan's Gini coefficient remains essentially constant, no sweeping statement about inequality trend in HPAEs seems warranted. In particular, Taiwan, Hong Kong and Singapore, with their U-shaped curves, are exhibiting a worsening distribution of income since the late 1970s or the early 1980s.

Even Korea and Japan, which show either declining or constant inequality during the 1980s according to Figure 3, may have actually undergone a worsening of income distribution in the same period. In Japan, the Gini coefficient estimated from the Survey of Income Redistribution rose from 0.35 in 1980 to 0.43 in 1989, and that estimated from the Household Survey rose from 0.26 in 1979 to 0.28 in 1991 [*Ishikawa, 1994*]. In the case of Korea, some recent studies have found inequality rising throughout the 1980s right up to the early 1990s [*Ahn, 1992; Adelman, 1995*]. The rise in inequality in Taiwan that began in the 1980s continued into the 1990s, surpassing the late 1960s level, according to the official estimates [*CEPD, 1995*].

Admittedly, there are a variety of estimates of the Gini coefficients, and it is beyond the scope of this paper to try to find the most reliable or

FIGURE 3

TREND OF INEQUALITY IN HPAEs, 1957–88

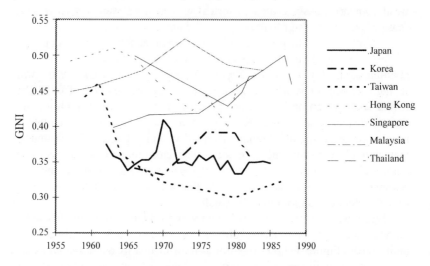

Source: Reproduced from Oshima [*1991: Fig.1, 120 and Fig.2, 122*].

Note: Original data sources are:

Japan: T. Mizoguchi, 'Economic, sociological and institutional factors related to changes in the size distribution of household income: Japan's experience in a century' (mimeo).

Taiwan: S.W.Y. Kuo, 'Income distribution in Taiwan'. For data for 1986-1987, *Survey of Personal Income Distribution in Taiwan [1986, 1987].*

Hong Kong: L.C. Chau, 'Economic growth and income distribution of Hong Kong since early 1950s'. For data for 1963-64, 1973-74 and 1979-80, Tzon-biau Lim, March 1985, 'Growth, equity and income distribution policies in Hong Kong' (mimeo).

Korea: Hakchung Choo, 1985, 'Estimation of size distribution of income and its sources of changes in Korea, 1982', *Korean Social Science Journal*, Vol.12. p.95.

Singapore: Gini ratios from V.V.B. Rao (Dept. of Economics, National University of Singapore), 1968, 'Income distribution in East Asian developing countries', *Asian-Pacific Economic Literature*, Vol.1, No.1, March p.28. Gini ratio for 1973 from V.V.B. Rao and M.K. Ramakrishnan, 1976, 'Income distribution in Singapore, 1966-1973', *Malayan Economic Review.*

Thailand: S. Hutaserani and S. Jitsuchon, 1988, 'Thailand's income distribution and poverty profile and other current situations', December, paper for TDRI Year-End Conference on income Distribution and Long-Term Development, 1988.

Malaysia: Gini ratio from V.V.B. Rao (Dept. of Economics, National University of Singapore), 1988, 'Income distribution in East Asian developing countries', *Asian-Pacific Economic Literature*, Vol.2, No.1, March. Data for 1984 from *Fifth Malaysian Plan 1986–1990*, p.100.

comparable estimates. The point here is simply that the World Bank's conclusion should not be accepted without further inquiries. The picture on the change in inequality can be very sensitive to the choice of data and the time period.[4]

(3) Explaining Low Inequality in the Super Three

The Miracle report argues that the HPAEs attained low inequality because of the 'principle of shared growth' [*World Bank, 1993, Ch.4*]. The governments of the HPAEs, it is argued, recognised the importance of including non-elites in sharing the benefits of growth and engaged in activist policies – policies to address ethnic inequalities, government provision of universal primary education, housing and health services, support for small- and medium-sized industries, etc. – to redress the inadequacies of the market system in distribution. This sounds nicer than the cold-blooded 'trickle-down' thesis, but is it true?

The presence of seemingly distribution-oriented policies does not explain much. It would be very difficult to come up with examples of governments that do not have any kind of distribution-improving, cosmetic or substantive, policies. What matters is the overall thrust of government policy rather than the existence of some programmes.[5] In looking at the big picture of the governments' proclivity to sharing the fruits of growth and protecting the poor, the share of government social expenditure is probably as good a measure as any. And by this standard the East Asian governments have invariably shown little such proclivity. In 1980, for instance, the share of central government expenditure on social security, housing and welfare was 21.1 per cent in Japan and 7.6 per cent in Singapore. This compares poorly with the other high-income economies' levels that range from 30 to 50 per cent; 7.5 per cent in Korea, 11.1 per cent in Taiwan, and 7.0 per cent in Malaysia; while the typical figures for the upper-middle income economies range from 20 to 30 per cent; 5.1 per cent in Thailand and 1.8 per cent in Indonesia, which are on the low side even by the standard of the poor countries [data from: *World Bank, 1995, Table 11; Ministry of Finance, 1995; CEPD, 1995*].

In fact, having debunked the myth of low inequality in the HPAEs except in the super three, we should no longer search for an explanation of low inequality that covers the entire HPAEs as a group. Instead, we must look for the distinguishing features of the super three that set them apart from the rest of the HPAEs. The land reform and the rapid expansion of employment in the modern sector seem to offer the most powerful explanations of the low inequality in the super three.

It is well known that Japan, Korea and Taiwan had thorough land reforms in the aftermath of the Second World War, and as a result have unusually egalitarian distribution of farmland. Post-war reforms in Japan also included the dissolution of the *zaibatsu* and the imposition of almost punitive wealth tax, with the highest marginal tax rate reaching 90 per cent [*Minami, 1996*]. In Korea, much real wealth was redistributed in the immediate post-war period through confiscation and selling-off of the former Japanese assets, inflation fighting measures that hit those who possessed financial wealth, and the extensive destruction of properties during the Korean War [*Adelman, 1995*]. Thus, the super three had one of the most egalitarian distributions of real and financial assets at the beginning of the high growth period.

The above historical condition is no doubt a crucial reason for the relatively egalitarian distribution of income in the super three, but it is far from being the end of the story for a number of reasons. First, it is possible to have relatively even distribution of land and yet still have high income inequality, if for example rural–urban income difference or some other unequalising factor is strong. Thailand is an example. It has considerably higher income inequality than Japan or Taiwan, although its distribution of land is more egalitarian than in the latter economies.[6] Second, because of the declining importance of agriculture in the super three – the agricultural shares of employment in these countries decreased to between two and 12 per cent in 1994 – land distribution is no longer such an important factor accounting for income equality. Third, a fundamental characteristic of capitalist development is its unevenness, as it tends to build on the best. Even if the initial distribution of assets is equal, capitalist development tends to produce highly concentrated asset distributions [*You, 1996*].[7] It is therefore necessary to explain how the initially low level of inequality was preserved through the prolonged period of rapid growth that brought about revolutionary changes in the structure of the economy.

This is precisely why the rapid expansion of employment in the modern sector is another crucial explanation of the low inequality in the super three. Employment expansion in labour-intensive export industries and consequent rises in real wages increased the incomes of the poor sections of the population, which had few assets other than labour [*Ranis and Fei, 1975; World Bank, 1987*]. This was a particularly powerful mechanism to hold inequality down at the earlier stage of rapid growth when there was substantial amount of open and disguised unemployment. While this was common to all the HPAEs, the super three attained the highest growth rates and therefore the most rapid job creation and wage increases. In doing so, they did not simply rely on a free trade strategy of emphasising labour-intensive exports based on comparative advantage.

The super three are in fact distinct from the rest of the HPAEs in that their governments vigorously pursued activist industrial policies with a mix of import substitution and export promotion. When we look at the pattern of employment expansion in the super three, we find that employment in the capital-intensive sector expanded as fast as that in the labour-intensive one in what has been called a 'dual-industrial growth' [*Ohno and Imaoka, 1987*]. In a recent paper analysing Korean wage inequality, Kim and Topel [*1995: 229*] find that 'sectors that employ relatively unskilled workers did not expand more rapidly than others. Instead, the data point to improvements in human capital as the major force that narrowed wage differences'. While sustained employment expansion and productivity growth have been important in maintaining 'growth with equity' in the super three, it is a process involving much more than free trade.

To the extent that the activist industrial policies were successful in promoting growth and creating jobs, they may have contributed to keeping the inequality levels low in the super three East Asian countries. Another aspect of the industrial policy may also be relevant here. The super three had a highly restrictive policy against foreign direct investment (FDI) as a part and parcel of their industrial policy. Many empirical studies have come to the conclusion that reliance on FDI has an adverse effect on income distribution [*Bornschier and Chase-Dunn, 1985; Tsai, 1995*]. This conclusion is also born out by the East Asian data; those HPAEs that have higher inequality than their income group median (Singapore, Hong Kong, Malaysia) all show very high FDI reliance, while those HPAEs that have lower inequality than their income group median (the super three) all have FDI reliance below the world average (see UNCTAD [*1993: Annex Table 3*] for data on FDI).

II. DISTRIBUTION OF INCOME AND CAPITAL ACCUMULATION IN EAST ASIA

To provide an account of the dynamic interaction between income distribution and growth in East Asia, the classical/Keynesian view that accords central importance to the role of profits as the source of, and the incentive for, accumulation seems to be an indispensable perspective. In the classical/Keynesian tradition income distribution is at least to some extent an institutionally determined exogenous variable, and capital accumulation and growth are influenced by the given distribution of income. The central aspect of income distribution here is that between wages and profits, because profits are saved to a much greater extent than wages and thus become the main source of accumulation.[8] In this perspective the rapid growth in East Asia is attributable primarily to the extraordinary rates of capital accumulation rather than efficient allocation of given resources.[9]

High share of profits may not be necessary for rapid accumulation, but most existing capitalist economies are so structured institutionally that it is. East Asian countries did manage to have high shares of profits, partly with the help of active government policies. They also distinguished themselves in successfully translating high profits into high savings and high business investment by a variety of policy measures and institutional structures, something many developing countries with high profit shares have failed to do. Furthermore, the relatively egalitarian distribution of household income in the super three was conducive to rapid accumulation of human capital.

(1) Income Distribution and Savings

In order to maintain rapid capital accumulation without running into inflation and balance of payment problems, it is essential to raise the domestic saving rate to a level close in the long run to the investment rate. The increase in the saving rates in East Asia, from the rather unremarkable levels of below 20 per cent in the 1960s to the extraordinary levels of 35 per cent or more in the 1990s, is therefore no doubt an important part of the success story. However, there has not been a satisfactory account of this [*Singh, 1995*].

According to the life-cycle hypothesis, the main determinants of the household saving rate are the interest rate, the demographic variables, the social security system and the growth rate.[10] In most time-series or cross-section studies, however, the only variable that performs consistently well is the growth rate (see, for example, Edwards [*1995*]). This suggests that the habit consumption hypothesis proposed by Marglin [*1984*] or the buffer stock saving behaviour put forward by Deaton [*1992*] may be more relevant than the life-cycle hypothesis in understanding household saving behaviour. At any rate, saying that the growth rate must be raised in order to increase the saving rate would not be a useful policy advice for a country trying to raise the saving rate in order to increase the growth rate. But it does mean – as Nam [*1990*] says in interpreting his conclusion that growth is the overwhelmingly important determinant of Korean savings – that deflationary adjustment policies, like high interest rate policy, may be self-defeating as deteriorating growth could sharply reduce national savings.

The Miracle report can only point to macroeconomic stability as the main reason for the high saving rates in East Asia. While it is hard to dispute that macroeconomic stability is generally conducive to savings and growth, two problems exist. First, it is very difficult to define precisely what macroeconomic stability is. At what level does inflation threaten stability, five per cent, 20 per cent or 50 per cent? How do we judge if the budget deficit is sustainable? This problem is confounded by the fact that, as Fischer [*1993: 21*] notes after reviewing the evidence, 'low inflation and small deficits are not necessary for high growth, over even quite long periods'. Second, there is also a reverse causality: macroeconomic stability is to a great extent a result of high savings.

It seems that the neoclassical emphasis on household savings is one of the reasons why the high saving rates in East Asia have not been properly understood. In a strictly neo-classical world, any increases in government savings and business retained earnings are exactly offset by an equivalent reduction in household savings on account of the Miller-Modigliani theorem and the Ricardian equivalence theorem. However, the econometric evidence as well as the reasoning based on the assumption of imperfect information suggest that they are not [*Malinvaud, 1986*]. Once we recognise the independent role of these institutional savings, in particular the connection between profits and business savings, there is no more mystery about high saving rates in East Asia.

Sectoral savings data in developing countries are hard to come by. Table 2 reports the available data, constructed from Honohan and Atiyas [*1989*] and supplemented by Taiwanese data calculated from national income accounts. It gives the five-year averages for sectoral savings, investment and surpluses in the early 1980s (three-year averages for some countries, late 1970s for others). It can be seen that the East Asian countries have unusually high business saving rates, but that their household and government saving rates are not particularly high. These economies, including China, have business saving rates higher than 8.3 per cent of GNP, while all the other advanced and developing countries, except the United Kingdom and Cameroon, have business saving rates lower than 6.2 per cent of GNP. Table 2 also shows that, between the East Asian averages and the non-East Asian averages, the figures are practically identical except for the significantly higher business saving rates and business investment rates in East Asia.

A high business saving rate may be due to a high share of business profits in the distribution of income and/or a high profit-retention ratio. Can we say then that the high rates of business savings in East Asia derive from the income distribution that is unusually favourable to profits? The answer is a qualified yes. All the East Asian countries have relatively high profit shares (equivalently, low wage shares), but almost a half the developing countries have profit shares similar to or higher than the East Asian level.

Table 3 gives summary information on the distribution of the wage share across countries. The wage share is measured by total employee earnings as a percentage of the manufacturing value added. This of course is not a proper measure of the wage share, since the employee earnings do not include the labour income of the self-employed, which can be quite large in developing countries. We could in principle estimate the imputed wage of the self-employed, but the required information to carry out the calculations

TABLE 2

SECTORAL SAVINGS AND INVESTMENT IN SELECTED COUNTRIES

	Country	Household		Business		Government		National Economy		
		Sh	Ih	Sb	Ib	Sg	Ig	Sd	Id	Sf
EA	China	12.54	5.53	14.05	22.13	5.95	5.69	32.54	33.35	0.81
	Korea	10.27	5.33	8.30	19.98	4.11	3.05	22.69	28.36	5.69
	Malaysia	19.69	2.90	9.13	16.28	-1.16	11.07	27.66	30.25	2.59
	Taiwan	13.7	..	12.0	..	6.2	4.1	31.9	26.9	-5.0
	Thailand	10.40	3.62	8.67	15.19	0.16	4.46	19.23	23.27	4.04
	Japan	16.92	7.76	10.83	15.56	6.43	8.34	34.18	31.66	-2.52
	East Asian average	13.92	5.03	10.50	17.83	3.61	6.12	28.03	28.97	0.94
Adv.	France	11.72	7.61	6.17	10.94	2.66	4.09	20.54	22.64	2.10
	Italy	21.34	7.42	4.13	6.95	-7.64	4.51	17.83	18.88	1.05
	UK	9.35	5.51	9.96	9.07	-0.64	2.74	18.67	17.32	-1.35
Dev.	Cameroon	4.43	0.41	9.23	18.66	9.36	6.72	23.02	25.79	2.77
	Colombia	8.58	5.07	5.46	10.43	2.06	4.62	16.10	20.12	4.02
	Côte d'Ivoire	4.09	2.99	3.36	12.33	14.40	11.62	21.85	26.94	5.09
	Ecuador	9.55	4.97	3.64	11.08	4.55	7.85	17.74	23.90	6.16
	India	16.59	10.0	1.91	3.13	4.64	11.24	23.14	24.36	1.23
	Philippines	10.04	0.97	3.28	10.24	4.44	8.08	17.76	19.28	1.52
	Portugal	24.12	10.28	0.05	16.93	-2.55	4.75	21.62	31.95	10.33
	Turkey	12.13	4.46	3.92	16.13	5.16	6.38	21.20	26.96	5.76
	Tunisia	6.66	4.34	5.88	20.42	9.55	5.07	22.09	29.83	7.74
	Non-East Asian average	11.58	5.34	4.75	12.17	3.83	6.48	20.13	24.00	3.87

Source: Calculated from Honohan and Atiyas [1989] and *Taiwan Statistical Data Book, 1995.*

Notes: Sh = household savings/GNP; Ih = household investment/GNP, etc.
Sd = Sh + Sb + Sg, Id = Ih + Ib + Ig, Sf = Id - Sd.
Figures are five-year averages for 1980-84, where available, or the closest period.

is lacking in many developing countries. We would have exactly the same problem if we were to use the share of the gross operating surplus in the value added from the national income accounts. Although for some countries direct survey data on the wage share are available, we chose the above measure for reasons of comparability and availability for a large number of countries. In order to minimise the problem of the self-employed sector, we made comparisons within the four income groups. However, except for the fact that the high-income economies have on the whole substantially higher wage shares, there is no systematic relationship between the earnings share and the level of income in the rest.

From Table 3 we find that Japan and Singapore among the high-income economies and Indonesia among the low-income economies have one of the lowest wage shares; the other HPAEs in the middle-income group have wage shares which are close to the group median values; and Hong Kong has one

TABLE 3
SHARE OF EARNINGS IN MANUFACTURING
VALUE ADDED IN HPAES AND THE WORLD

Income group	1970	1989–91
Low incom economies:		
Number of countries	20	14
Range	16–54	18–44
Median, Average	30,32	31,31
Indonesia	26	19
Lower-middle income economies:		
Number of countries	22	20
Range	19–45	15–51
Median, Average	31,32	28,30
Thailand	24	28
Upper-middle income economies:		
Number of countries	11	16
Range	22–46	2–77
Median, Average	31,32	27,31
Malaysia	28	27
Korea	25	29
High income economies:		
Number of countries	19	21
Range	32–56	27–60
Median, Average	49,48	42,44
Hong Kong	..	55
Singapore	36	32
Japan	32	33

Source: Calculated from *World Development Report, 1994*, Table 7.

Note: The above table gives figures for 1970, 1989, 1990 and 1991. The figures for the last

of the highest wage shares. On the other hand, the wage shares in all the HPAEs, with the exception of Hong Kong, are all below the group averages.

The observation of the relatively high profit shares and business saving rates in East Asia does not by itself establish the causality. We may explore the correlation between the two variables across countries, but the paucity of the sectoral savings data prevents this. On the other hand, since a substantial part of household savings is either business savings of small establishments or personal savings from profit-related income [*Akyüz and Gore, 1995*], we may look at the correlation between the aggregate savings and the profit share. Among the advanced countries, there is indeed a close correlation between these variables [*OECD, 1990*]. However, we should not expect such a close correlation for developing countries, given the fact that there are too many countries where high profits fail to find their way into savings. For example, Kaldor [*1964*] found that the chief problem in Chile was precisely that high profits were not generating much savings because of the conspicuous consumption of the rich. Countries such as Colombia, Ecuador and the Philippines also have low saving rates (see Table 2) but their wage shares are also comparatively low.

The high saving rates in East Asia must be attributed not only to profit-oriented income distribution but to the fact that somehow an unusually large proportion of profits was saved.[11] The most fundamental factor in this is investment demand, since the business saving rate is closely related to the need for investment funds. Having noted the fundamental importance of buoyant animal spirits, we must also recognise that, at least in part, the corporate saving rate is influenced by institutional settings and policies. Both Japan and Korea have a corporate financing system with heavy reliance on bank loans and the relatively insignificant role of the stock market, with the controlling shares in the hands of other firms within the group or with close business relations. This has allowed the firms to retain high portions of profits instead of paying dividends. At the same time preferential tax treatment of capital gains over distributed income has acted as an incentive to retain profits.

East Asian governments also utilised various policies to promote household savings – whether the household income out of which savings are made is profit-related or not. They restricted consumption in various ways, including restrictions on importation of consumer goods and suppressing consumer financing (for example, requiring a large down-payment for housing loans) [*UNCTAD, 1997*]. This was especially vigorous in Korea, where the government periodically mounted campaigns for belt-tightening and demonised what it deemed luxury consumption and conspicuous consumption. Furthermore, East Asian countries complemented the consumption restriction policy by tight foreign exchange controls to prevent capital flight before they were relieved of the balance-of-payment problems. Finally, the East Asian governments created financial institutions and schemes such as postal savings, forced saving schemes for school children, incentive measures for workers' savings, etc., to maximise mobilisation of savings.

(2) Profits and Investment

It goes without saying that it is more important to maintain high rates of investment than to generate high rates of saving. While investment can create savings to some extent, savings do not create investment. On the contrary, if the high saving rate is not matched by vigorous investment demand, the result will be declining output and stagnation and, consequently, a shrinking volume of savings. If a high profit share gives rise to a high saving rate, therefore, it can be bliss or a disaster, depending on whether the high profit share also induces a high rate of investment. This point relates to the controversy on the relationship between income distribution and growth, between the classical and Keynesian approaches.

The classical position is that a higher saving rate stemming from a higher share of profits naturally leads to a higher rate of investment and growth. However, the Keynesian 'paradox of thrift' says that a higher saving rate means lower effective demand and hence lower output, and the latter, via the accelerator principle, will cause investment demand to fall. Describing what they call the 'profit–investment nexus' in East Asia, Akyüz and Gore [1995] argue that high profits were the key to the rapid growth in East Asia, thus taking a position close to the classical one. On the other hand, taking the stagnationist position, Dutt [1984] points to the high share of profits as a cause of low growth in India.

Why would high profits lead to rapid accumulation in some countries and stagnation in others? Is it because some economies are supply-constrained (classical) and others demand-constrained (Keynesian)? It is not necessary to make such an arbitrary assumption. As Bhaduri and Marglin [1990] have shown, the classical position that a higher profit share leads to a higher rate of accumulation does not require the classical assumption that the economy is supply-constrained. Even in a demand-constrained economy, the classical result may obtain provided that investment demand is sufficiently responsive to profitability (a case that Bhaduri and Marglin call 'exhilarationist' as opposed to 'stagnationist').[12] Apart from the responsiveness of investment demand to profitability, the presence of an intercept, that is, other determinants than profitability, in the investment function may explain the diversity of the relationship between distribution and accumulation. Investment in East Asia may be greater because of the entrepreneurs' higher animal spirits or for some institutional reasons.

A high profit share in the distribution of income is not a sufficient condition for rapid accumulation of capital. For the latter it is necessary to have strong investment demand – very responsive to profitability in the case of an exhilarationist regime or with a large intercept in the case of a stagnationist one. As with savings, therefore, a satisfactory account of the high rates of investment in East Asia must explain the ways in which the high profits motivated vigorous investment activities instead of complacence in the *status quo* or indulgence in speculation.

It is here that the role of the government becomes pivotal. Historically speaking, modern economic growth came along with the emergence of the 'progressive' bourgeois class, with a strong investment drive, and the problem of underdevelopment was precisely the lack of such a class [*Baran, 1957*]. The government must therefore step in. In an extensive survey of developing country growth experience, Reynolds [*1986*] finds that the single most important moment for the 'take-off' is the emergence of a development-oriented state. The government can jump-start the investment process not only by public investment but also through establishment of the appropriate financial system to mobilise and channel the savings into investment and providing incentives for private investment. As the World Bank [*1993*] observes, the more successful countries like the HPAEs are the ones that succeeded in generating buoyancy of private investment demand (see Table 2). Private investment of course responds to profit expectations, for which both profitability and risks of investment matter. And these were not left by the East Asian governments for the market forces to determine.

First, a number of policies were aimed at improving the profitability of investment, particularly in the strategic industries chosen by the government. The most important in this regard was the policies to reduce the cost of investment by such means as low interest rate policy loans, low import duties for investment goods, allowing accelerated depreciation for tax purposes, provision of industrial infrastructure, etc. Another element was the suppression of independent unionism to maintain competitive wage rates (that is, keeping real wages from rising above the productivity growth rates) and foster a good investment climate.

Second, policies to reduce investment risks take on a particular significance when the economy is diversifying into unknown areas of activities in a process of catching-up and industrial upgrading [*Chang, 1994*]. This is in the area of industrial policy. East Asian governments reduced risks by coordinating private sector investment according to their carefully planned development strategy. This coordination went beyond simply indicating which areas to invest in to regulating the overall amount of investment to prevent excessive investment and organising recession cartels to protect profits. All of this reduces risks considerably, although it does not eliminate risks altogether, as instances of failure demonstrate. Combined with various financial and other supports, risk-reducing coordination policies produce powerful incentives for investment.[13]

(3) Household Distribution of Income and Human Capital Accumulation

In the above we explored the connection between the functional distribution of income and physical capital accumulation. There is also some recent literature concerning the effect of exogenous income distribution on human capital accumulation. The relevant distribution here is the household distribution.

Given the imperfections in the capital market and the lumpiness of the educational investment, it is argued that the distribution of income decides how many in the population can invest in human capital [*Galor and Zeira, 1993*]. High inequality may be conducive to growth at low levels of income, but once a certain level of income is reached lower inequality allows more people to invest in human capital, and thus produces higher output growth [*Perotti, 1993*]. *The Miracle* report, which makes much of human capital accumulation as an explanatory variable for the high growth in East Asia, also makes the point that egalitarian income distribution was an important reason for the rapid increase in the level of education.

It is hard to dispute the plausibility of the virtuous circle linking egalitarian income distribution and human capital accumulation. However, such a virtuous circle cannot operate unless demand for educated workers rises at a pace similar to the rise in education [*Singh, 1994*]. To the extent that the virtuous circle argument is correct, it is correct in East Asia only because East Asia was successful in generating rapid growth in output and rapid accumulation of physical capital, embodying ever more sophisticated technologies that demand more educated workers.

III. HIGH PROFIT SHARE AND LOW INEQUALITY:
    A CONUNDRUM?

Income distribution in the East Asian super three is characterised by high profit shares in the functional distribution of income and low inequality in the size distribution of income, which has had favourable consequences for physical capital accumulation and human capital formation, respectively. Since a high profit share and low inequality normally do not go together, a question arises as to how it was possible for the super three East Asian countries to have both at the same time [*Akyüz and Gore, 1995*]. This is the question we now turn to. In searching for the answers, we first examine the evidence on the distribution of income-generating wealth and the distribution of wages, and then consider some other factors.[14]

(1) Distribution of Wealth

It seems quite clear that part of the answer lies in the unusually low inequality in the distribution of assets. Table 4 presents some of the available evidence on wealth distribution. Although there may be data comparability problems between Japan and Korea on the one hand and France and the United States on the other, the difference in the Gini coefficients of wealth distribution in these two groups of countries is sufficiently large to suggest that the East Asian wealth distribution is more egalitarian. The Gini coefficient for the distribution of gross assets is 0.71 for France and 0.77 for the United States, while it is only 0.58 for Korea. For the distribution of net worth, the Gini is 0.69 for France and 0.75 for the United States, but in Japan only 0.52 in 1984 and, even after a serious deterioration during the bubble economy, 0.64 in 1989. Another revealing piece of information is that the top five per cent owns 43 per cent of wealth in the United States [Kessler and Wolff, 1991], while in Korea the top ten per cent owns as much [Kwon et al., 1992].[15]

TABLE 4

GINI COEFFICIENT FOR WEALTH DISTRIBUTION IN FOUR COUNTRIES

	France 1980	US 1983			Japan 1984	Japan 1989	Korea 1988
I. Assets	0.71	0.77	I. Assets				0.579
1. Owner-occupied housing	0.32	0.43	1. Land		0.553	0.721	
2. Other real estate	0.56	0.75	2. Housing		0.620	0.602	
3. Unincorporated business	0.49	0.79	3. Consumer durables		0.268	0.371	
4. Currency and demand deposits	0.65	0.74	4. Real assets (=1+2+3)		0.529	0.677	0.596
5. Time deposits and savings accounts	0.70	0.77	5. Financial assets		0.535	0.564	0.770
II. Liabilities	0.61	0.68	II. Liabilities		0.775	0.794	
III. Net worth	0.69	0.75	III. Net worth		0.519	0.639	

Source: Kessler and Wolff [1991] for France and the United States, Takayama and Arita [1994] for Japan, and Kwon et al. [1992] for Korea.

Note: For France and the United States, other items of financial assets that are not reported here include securities, shares, insurance and pension reserves, and the Gini coefficients are calculated for owners of the assets concerned.

What are the reasons, then, for the unusually even distribution of wealth in the East Asian economies? For one thing, the evenness of the initial distribution of land and other real and financial assets may be exerting a long-lasting effect (although, according to the information given in Table 4, land distribution in Japan no longer retains a particularly egalitarian character). Another reason for the low inequality of wealth distribution may be found in the saving behaviour of different income classes. As noted by Kwon *et al.* [*1992*], the saving rates of low income households in the East Asian countries are surprisingly high, especially in Japan and Taiwan. The relatively low Gini coefficient for the distribution of financial assets in Japan is a consequence of such behaviour. The Japanese may have a point when they boast that theirs is capitalism without capitalists.

Clearly, the two reasons given above are not unrelated. The less the difference between the savings propensities of high and low income households, the longer the effects of the initially egalitarian distribution of assets will last. It is also obvious that an egalitarian distribution of wages will have similar influences in terms of prolonging the initially favourable distribution of wealth as well as improving the size distribution at a given point in time.

(2) Distribution of Wages

The evidence on wage inequality is not so clear. Davis [*1992*] presents an analysis of the wage differential among men in five countries – Korea, France, the United States, the United Kingdom and Canada. He shows that the overall wage inequality among men in Korea was initially quite high compared to the advanced countries, but that it has decreased over time. In the 1980s it became lower than in the United States and France, although higher than in the United Kingdom and Canada, in the upper half of the distribution, and lower than in the United States and Canada, although higher than in the United Kingdom and France, in the bottom half of the distribution. Another piece of available evidence on cross national comparison of wage inequality is in Katz *et al.* [*1995*], where wage inequality among men and among women are separately analysed for Japan, the United States, the United Kingdom and France. It shows that Japan had the lowest wage inequality for both sexes among the four countries, although the United Kingdom also had low inequality in the 1970s. However, the overall wage inequality for all – both male and female – workers in Japan may not be as favourable as that, since the wage difference between male and female workers in Japan is by far the highest among the advanced countries. It is no surprise that Rowthorn [*1991*] finds the inter-industry wage dispersion, when calculated by taking the male and female wages in the same industry as separate observations, to be the highest in

Japan among 17 advanced countries. A similar tendency must exist for Korea, which also has an extremely high gender wage differential.

From the above discussion we can only conclude that wage distributions in Japan and Korea are not particularly equal in comparison to advanced Western countries. Comparison with other developing countries is difficult owing to the paucity of relevant data. Davis [1992] compares educational wage differences in eight countries – the United States, Canada, the United Kingdom, Japan, Korea, Brazil, Colombia and Venezuela. It is shown that the educational wage differences in Japan declined steeply until the mid-1970s and continued the downward trend in the 1980s, unlike in the United States or the United Kingdom and, as a result, is significantly lower than in both these countries as well as Canada. They also declined sharply in the late 1980s in Korea, reaching levels comparable to the Anglo-Saxon countries. These developments owe probably to the increase in the relative supply of educated labour [Kim and Topel, 1995] as well as to the rapid tightening up of the labour market, which has a tendency to narrow wage differences between skilled and unskilled workers [Blank and Blinder, 1986]. Latin American countries – Brazil, Colombia and Venezuela – also had declining wage differences across educational groups, with roughly similar levels to those of Korea.

In conclusion, we do not find strong evidence of more equal wage distribution in East Asia, either in Japan against other advanced countries or in Korea against Latin American countries. This finding may be taken as strengthening the earlier assertion that it is the unusually egalitarian distribution of wealth in the East Asian countries that explains the low income inequality, in spite of high profit shares in those countries. There is another possibility, however, which relates to wage-earning opportunities. The same degree of wage inequality across individuals may be associated with different wage inequalities across households, depending on how widespread employment opportunities are. The rapid expansion of employment, accompanied by a substantial rise in the participation rate, and the near-full employment conditions in the super three strongly suggest that employment opportunities are more widely available there. Therefore, it seems likely that if, for example, the distribution of wage income across households is compared between East Asian and Latin American countries, East Asian distribution would be less unequal than Latin American distribution, despite the fact that wage inequality is similar in the two regions.

(3) Other Considerations

There may well be some other factors that explain the puzzle. First, as the World Bank [1993] argues, the urban-rural income differential may be lower and human capital distribution more equal in East Asia. However, there is simply no good evidence that these factors make a substantial difference.[16]

Second, another point the World Bank makes, that the presence of relatively large and vibrant small-scale businesses reduces overall income inequality, may be of some relevance, especially in Taiwan, and may be related to the savings behaviour and assets distribution in East Asia.

Finally and most importantly, the fact that corporate profits are retained to a greater extent in East Asia may be partly the reason for the coexistence of high profit shares and low inequality. Since retained corporate profits are not reflected in the household income, the effect of a higher profit share on the size distribution of income will be mitigated as the retention rate rises. Indeed, some recent studies of income distribution in Japan and Korea show that inequality increases dramatically when capital gains are included in the household income.[17]

IV. GROWTH WITH EQUITY: MAKING SENSE OF THE EAST ASIAN EXPERIENCE

This section attempts to wrap up our discussion on the East Asian experience with income distribution and growth and draw some lessons, both theoretical and practical.

It is convenient to start from the age-old debate about the trade-off between growth and equity. One argument in favour of the existence of such a trade-off relates to our discussion in section II: a higher rate of growth goes with a higher share of profits, which implies, other things being equal, a more unequal distribution of income. This logic is depicted in Figure 4, where a downward-sloping growth-equity (g-e) curve in the first quadrant is generated from the supposed positive relationship between growth and the profit share (g-π curve) in the second quadrant and the negative relationship between the profit share and equity (π-e curve) in the fourth quadrant.

However, there are serious flaws in the above argument. In the short run, it is quite possible for an economy to be stagnationist; that is, a negative relationship may prevail between the profit share and the growth rate. In such a case, there would be no trade-off between growth and equity. To the contrary, a higher growth rate would be associated with an improving income distribution. It might therefore be tempting to interpret the East Asian experience with growth with equity as an instance of wage-led growth in a stagnationist regime, as opposed to profit-led growth. However, given the limits to capacity utilisation, it is unlikely that such a wage-led growth can be sustained in the long run [*Skott, 1989*]. Moreover, as we

FIGURE 4

GROWTH-EQUITY TRADE-OFFS

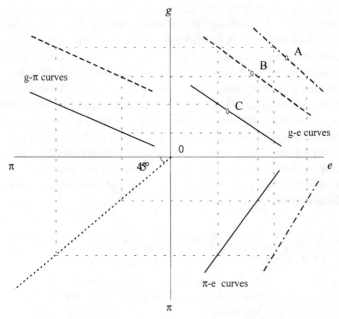

discussed earlier, high profits did play a crucial role in enabling rapid capital accumulation and growth in East Asia.

Another objection to the simplistic growth–equity trade-off based on profit-led growth is that, in the long run, it is absurd to suppose that other things will remain unchanged. With the passage of time, a number of institutional and market factors that determine the position of the g-π curve and the π-e curve are likely to change. In particular, the diversity of institutional and structural factors makes it extremely unlikely that the trade-off will be found in cross-section data. We now relate the latter point to the main arguments of the previous sections.

First, in section II we have argued that the East Asian countries distinguished themselves not so much by high profit shares as by the effective institutions and policies with which they succeeded in translating high profits into high savings and investment. In other words, the location of the g-π curve in East Asia was above that in most other countries. As the dotted lines in Figure 4 show, the growth–equity trade-off, while still there, becomes less agonising: compared to the countries on the original trade-off curve, it is possible to have both a higher rate of growth and a more equitable distribution of income.

Second, as we discussed in section III, there are a variety of factors that may associate different levels of inequality for a given profit share. In the case of the East Asian super three the distribution of wealth, among other things, may have caused inequality to be relatively low, even at quite high levels of the profit share. The broken lines in Figure 4 indicate that this would further shift the g-e curve away from the origin.

The moral of the above analysis is threefold. First, it is neither appealing nor necessary to discard the classical/Keynesian view of the relationship between income distribution and growth in trying to understand the unusual achievement of East Asia in combining rapid growth with a relatively equitable distribution of income. In terms of Figure 4, it may be understood as being on a point like A instead of B or C. Second, it follows that it is important to analyse the institutional and policy factors which put the g-π curve and the π-e curve in a more outward position than usual when we try to understand the East Asian achievement. Third, as a practical policy lesson, the East Asian experience suggests that the growth-equity trade-off may be alleviated by either a one-shot wealth redistribution, such as land reform, or measures to ensure that the bulk of profits are saved and reinvested.

V. CONCLUSION

This study began with an examination of the empirical evidence on income inequality in the HPAEs and found that only the super three – Japan, Korea and Taiwan – may be characterised as having unusually low inequality. In the subsequent sections we have tried to understand how it was possible for these countries to combine low inequality with rapid growth. The picture that emerges may be summarised as follows:

(1) The super three started the rapid growth phase with an exceptionally egalitarian distribution of real and financial assets as a result of post-war reforms.

(2) The rapid growth of income was based on rapid accumulation of capital as well as rapid expansion of employment.

(3) High profit shares played a crucial role in the accumulation process, both by generating high saving rates and by inducing high rates of investment. Even though high profits are not a sufficient condition for rapid growth, the East Asian super three achieved rapid accumulation because they complemented high profits with effective institutions and policies which translated them into savings and investment.

(4) High profit shares were compatible with relatively low inequality in the

size distribution of income, primarily because the wealth distribution was relatively even as a result of the highly egalitarian initial distribution and, especially in Japan and Taiwan, because of the unusual savings behaviour of the low-income households.

(5) Although the wage distribution in the super three is not particularly even, the rapid employment expansion and the attainment of near-full employment probably mean that the wage-earning opportunities are more widely distributed across households.

One uneasy implication of the above picture is that the future prospects of income distribution in East Asia are not so sanguine. The favourable influence of the initial wealth distribution will only diminish over time, and it will become harder and harder to expand employment from the already high levels. Indeed, there is evidence of a rising concentration of wealth, markedly so during the bubble period of the late 1980s, in all of the super three countries. This trend is also consistent with the observation that income inequality rose during the 1980s in Japan and Taiwan, and also in Korea by some accounts. These governments, therefore, need to pay more attention to improving income distribution in the future.

NOTES

1. As reported in an earlier version, using the ratio of the income shares of the richest ten per cent and the poorest 40 per cent of the population as the inequality measure does not change our findings in any significant way.
2. High growth is defined as a growth rate of five per cent or above in terms of the average annual GDP growth rate during 1980-92, the period in which most of the income distribution data are taken. A growth rate of 2.5 per cent or above but below 5 per cent is defined as medium growth, and a growth rate below 2.5 per cent low growth.
3. This is an important critique of World Bank [1993] since it advises other developing countries to follow the South-East Asian model rather than the super three. This recommendation is based on two arguments: first, the economic performance in terms of growth and equity is roughly the same in both areas; second, the institutional requirement of the interventionist East Asian model is too much for other developing countries. However, it turns out that the performance of the South-East Asian members of the HPAEs is inferior to East Asia both in terms of growth and, especially, in terms of income distribution.
4. Another example of this sensitivity is found in Sundrum [1990: 121]. Looking at an earlier period, he finds only Taiwan to be an exemplary case of low inequality combined with declining inequality. Other HPAEs are found to have either increasing inequality or mixed results.
5. A case in point is the Korean industrial policy. As is well known, the Korean government supported the giant business groups, *chaebol*, with huge amounts of subsidies. This policy was highly detrimental to the small- and medium-sized firms. In particular, the policy loans that went to *chaebol* firms swallowed up much of the bank loans, forcing the small- and medium-sized firms to rely on the much more expensive curb market loans. However, the Korean government also ran programmes to help the small- and medium-sized firms at the same time. Needless to say, the latter were quantitatively rather insignificant when compared to the support given to *chaebol*. See You [1995] for the overall thrust of the Korean government's policy toward growth and income distribution.

6. See the data given in Sundrum [*1990: 185*]. Jomo has suggested that it might be because there are large differences in the quality of land in Thailand. The poor farmers in the North-East region may own land, but the productivity of land there is much below than in other regions.

7. Adelman [*1995: 10*] asserts that 'by 1973 the distribution of real and financial assets [in Korea] was no longer even. ... [It] had become more like that of a typical developing country'. However, she does not give any quantitative evidence. In section III of this study, we examine some evidence suggesting that the distribution of wealth in the super three tended to be relatively equal, even as late as in the 1980s.

8. However, note that the life-cycle hypothesis or its growth theoretic incarnation – the overlapping generations model – implies exactly the opposite.

9. Young [*1995*] makes the same argument based on growth accounting.

10. However, the implication of the life-cycle hypothesis on the effect of growth on savings is not unambiguous. In a growing economy, on the one hand, workers' savings will increase relative to retirees' dissavings, and thereby raise the aggregate savings. On the other hand, workers may anticipate rising future incomes and increased consumption, as noted by Bosworth [*1993*].

11. While high profits are not sufficient to generate high savings, they are not necessary either. As Marglin [*1975*] observes, individuals may not be trusted to save much of their income, so large organisations such as business firms and pension systems or the state must play a substantial role here. Which organisations are to be utilised is a political decision. For example, the Nordic countries have relied on government savings rather uniquely among the advanced countries [*Kosonen, 1992*]. It might be recalled that the Swedish trade union economists, Meidner and Rehn, argued that 'democratically' enforced government savings must replace the 'undemocratic' profit-based (forced) savings.

12. See You [*1994*] for the exact conditions for this to happen. It also discusses the possibility of non-linearity in the relationship between the accumulation rate and the profit share, which can arise, for example, if investment is highly responsive to profitability when profitability is low, but is relatively unresponsive when it is already high. In this case, a stagnationist economy may well have a higher accumulation rate than an exhilarationist one.

13. This assessment of risk-reducing policies is not incompatible with the view that the underlying cause of the exhange crisis of 1997 is overinvestment. These policies led to the government's assumption of investment risks, which reduced individual firms' risks radically but not the systemic risks. When the government plan is conceived or ineffectively enforced, the systemic risks are actually amplified.

14. Note that the socialist economies used to have a highly egalitarian income distribution combined with high investment rates financed by the socialist equivalent of profits, the planned surplus, because they had a highly egalitarian distribution of wealth and wages.

15. Similar Gini's for Korea, France and the United States in Table 4 do not imply that distribution in Korea is as unequal as in France and the United States. First, the French and the US Gini's for other financial assets that are not reported in the table, such as financial securities and corporate stock shares, are much higher than those reported. Second, as their Gini's are calculated only for those who own the respective assets, they substantially underestimate the overall inequality.

16. For instance, Table 4.12 of Sundrum [*1990*] shows that in terms of the ratio of agricultural income to non-agricultural income Korea was worse than Malaysia, Colombia, Turkey and even Mexico in 1970, when its share of agricultural labour force was, at 50 per cent, comparable to the comparator countries. Also, the above comparison between Korea and Latin American countries in terms of educational wage differentials casts doubts on the claim that more equal distribution of education was the decisive factor in bringing down inequality in Korea.

17. See UNCTAD [*1997*]. See also Kwon *et al.* [*1992*] for Korea, and Tachibanaki and Yagi [*1994*] for Japan.

REFERENCES

Adelman, I., 1995, 'Social Development in Korea, 1953-1993', paper presented at the KDI Conference on 'The Korean Economy, 1945–95: Performance and Vision for the 21st Century', Seoul.

Ahn, K., 1992, 'Trends in the Size Distribution of Income in Korea', *Korean Social Science Journal*, Vol.18.

Akyüz, Y. and C. Gore, 1995, 'The Investment-Profits Nexus in East Asian Industrialization', *World Development*, Vol.24, No.3.

Baran, P., 1957, *The Political Economy of Growth*, Harmondsworth: Penguin.

Bhaduri, A. and S. Marglin, 1990, 'Unemployment and the Real Wage: Economic Basis for Contesting Political Ideologies', *Cambridge Journal of Economics*, Vol.14, No.4.

Blank, R. and A. Blinder, 1986, 'Macroeconomics, Income Distribution, and Poverty', in S. Danziger (ed.), *Antipoverty Policies: What Works and What Does Not*, Cambridge, MA: Harvard University Press.

Bornschier, V. and C. Chase-Dunn, 1985, *Transnational Corporations and Underdevelopment*, New York: Praeger Press.

Bosworth, B., 1993, *Savings and Investment in the Open Economy*, Washington, DC: The Brookings Institution.

CEPD, 1995, *Taiwan Statistical Data Book, 1995*, Republic of China: Council for Economic Planning and Development.

Chang, H-J., 1994, *The Political Economy of Industrial Policy*, London: Macmillan.

Davis, S.J., 1992, 'Cross-country Patterns of Change in Relative Wages', in O. Blanchard and S. Fischer (eds)., *NBER Macroeconomics Annual 1992*, Cambridge, MA: The MIT Press.

Deaton, A.S., 1992, *Understanding Consumption*, Oxford: Clarendon Press.

Dutt, A., 1984, 'Stagnation, Income Distribution and Monopoly Power', *Cambridge Journal of Economics*, Vol.8, No.1.

Edwards, S., 1995, 'Why are Saving Rates so Different Across Countries? An International Comparative Analysis', *NBER Working Paper*, No.5097, Cambridge, MA: The MIT Press.

Fischer, S., 1993, 'The Role of Macroeconomic Factors in Growth', *NBER Working Paper*, No.4565, Cambridge, MA: The MIT Press.

Galor, O. and Joseph Zeira, 1993, 'Income Distribution and Macroeconomics', *Review of Economic Studies*, Vol.60, pp.35–52.

Honohan, P. and I. Atiyas, 1989, 'Intersectoral Financial Flows in Developing Countries', *World Bank PPR Working Paper*, No.164, Washington, DC: World Bank.

Ishikawa, T., 1994, 'Distribution of Income and Wealth in Japan', in T. Ishikawa (ed.), *Nihonno Shotokuto Funo Bunpai* (Distribution of Wealth and Income in Japan), Tokyo: University of Tokyo Press.

Kaldor, N., 1964, 'Economic Problems of Chile', in *Essays on Economic Policy II*, London: Duckworth.

Katz, L.F. *et al.*, 1995, 'A Comparison of Changes in the Structure of Wages in Four OECD Countries', in R.B. Freeman and L.F. Katz (eds.), *Differences and Changes in Wage Structure*, Chicago, IL: University of Chicago Press.

Kessler, D. and E.N. Wolff, 1991, 'A Comparative Analysis of Household Wealth Patterns in France and the United States', *Review of Income and Wealth*, Series 37, No.3.

Keynes, J.M., 1919, *The Economic Consequences of Peace*, London: Macmillan.

Kim, D-I. and R.H. Topel, 1995, 'Labor Markets and Economic Growth: Lessons from Korea's Industrialization, 1970–1990', in R.B. Freeman and L.F. Katz (eds.), *Differences and Changes in Wage Structure*, Chicago, IL: University of Chicago Press.

Kosonen, K., 1992, 'Saving and Economic Growth from a Nordic Perspective', in J. Pekkarinen *et al.* (eds.), *Social Corporatism: A Superior Economic System?*, Oxford: Clarendon Press.

Kwon, S. *et al.*, 1992, *Realities of Distributional Inequality and Main Policy Agenda* (Punbae Pulgyundengui Siltaewa Chuyo Chongchaek Kwaje), Seoul: KDI Press.

Malinvaud, E., 1986, 'Pure Profits as Forced Saving', *Scandinavian Journal of Economics*, Vol.88, No.1.

Marglin, S., 1975, 'What do Bosses do? The Origins and Functions of Hierarchy in Capitalist

Production, Part 2', *Review of Radical Political Economics*, Vol.7.

Marglin, S., 1984, *Growth, Distribution and Prices*, Cambridge, MA: Harvard University Press.

Minami, R., 1996, 'Income Inequality in the Economic Development of Japan: An Evaluation of the Kuznets Hypothesis', mimeo, Kunitachi, Japan: Hitotsubashi University.

Ministry of Finance, 1995, *Zaisei Tokei* (Public Finance Statistics), Statistics Division, Japan.

Mizoguchi, T. (ed.), 1991, *Making Economies More Efficient and More Equitable: Factors Determining Income Distribution*, Tokyo: Kinokuniya/Oxford: Oxford University Press.

Nam, S-W., 1990, 'A Sectoral Accounting Approach to National Savings Applied to Korea', *Journal of Development Economics*, Vol.33, No.1.

OECD, 1990, *Historical Statistics, 1960–88*, Paris.

Ohno, K. and H. Imaoka, 1987, 'The Experience of Dual-Industrial Growth: Korea and Taiwan', *The Developing Economies*, Vol.25, No.4.

Oshima, H.T., 1991, 'Kuznets' Curve and Asian Income Distribution', in Mizoguchi [*1991*].

Perkins, D.H., 1994, 'There are at least Three Models of East Asian Development', *World Development*, Vol.22, No.4.

Perotti, R., 1993, 'Political Equilibrium, Income Distribution and Growth', *Review of Economic Studies*, Vol.60, pp.755–76.

Ranis, G. and J. Fei, 1975, 'A Model of Growth and Employment in the Open Dualistic Economy: The Cases of Korea and Taiwan', in F. Stewart (ed.), *Employment, Income Distribution and Development*, London: Frank Cass.

Reynolds, L., 1986, *Economic Growth in the Third World*, New Haven, CT: Yale University Press.

Rowthorn, R., 1991, 'Wage Dispersion and Employment in OECD Countries', in Mizoguchi [*1991*].

Singh, A., 1994, '"Openness" and the "Market-friendly" Approach to Development: Learning the Right Lessons from Development Experience', *World Development*, Vol.22, No.4.

Singh, A., 1995, 'How did East Asia Grow so Fast?', *UNCTAD Discussion Papers*, No.97, Geneva: UNCTAD.

Skott, P., 1989, *Conflict and Effective Demand in Economic Growth*, Cambridge: Cambridge University Press.

Sundrum, R.M., 1990, *Income Distribution in Less Developed Countries*, London: Routledge.

Tachibanaki, T. and T. Yagi, 1994, 'Recent Trends in Income Distribution', in T. Ishikawa (ed.), *Nihonno Shotokuto Funo Bunpai* (Distribution of Wealth and Income in Japan), Tokyo: University of Tokyo Press.

Takayama, K. and F. Arita, 1994, 'Distribution of Household Assets and its Changes', in T. Ishikawa (ed.), *Nihonno Shotokuto Funo Bunpai* (Distribution of Wealth and Income in Japan), Tokyo: University of Tokyo Press.

Tsai, P-L., 1995, 'Foreign Direct Investment and Income Inequality: Further Evidence', *World Development*, Vol.23, No.3.

UNCTAD, 1993, *World Investment Report, 1993*, New York and Geneva: UNCTAD.

UNCTAD, 1997, *Trade and Development Report, 1997*, New York and Geneva: UNCTAD.

World Bank, 1987, *World Development Report, 1987*, New York: Oxford University Press.

World Bank, 1993, *The East Asian Miracle: Economic Growth and Public Policy*, New York: Oxford University Press.

World Bank, 1994, *World Development Report, 1994*, New York: Oxford University Press.

World Bank, 1995, *World Development Report, 1995*, New York: Oxford University Press.

You, J-I., 1994, 'Macroeconomic Structure, Endogenous Technical Change and Growth', *Cambridge Journal of Economics*, Vol.18, No.2.

You, J-I., 1995, 'A Reflection on the Korean Miracle: Toward a New Concept of Development', *Ritsumeikan Journal of International Relations and Area Studies*, Vol.8.

You, J-I., 1996, 'Capitalism and Inequality: A Complete Model of Endogenous Distribution of Income', mimeo, Kyoto, Japan: Ritsumeikan University.

Young, A., 1995, 'The Tyranny of Numbers: Confronting the Statistical Realities of the East Asian Growth Experience', *Quarterly Journal of Economics*, Vol.110, No.3, pp.641–80.

Transferable Lessons?
Re-examining the Institutional Prerequisites
of East Asian Economic Policies

PETER EVANS

*Competing theories of East Asian economic policy share the
assumption that a highly capable, coherent economic bureaucracy,
closely connected to, but still independent of, the business
community, has been an essential institutional prerequisite for
successful policy formation and implementation. In East Asia these
institutional prerequisites were constructed in a variety of concrete
forms with great difficulty and imperfect results. As long as the
idea of 'transferable lessons' is understood as an invitation to
indigenous innovation that takes advantage of the underlying
analytical logic of East Asian institutions, other countries can reap
important benefits from East Asia's experience.*

Prior to the East Asian financial crisis, trying to extract transferable lessons
from East Asia was a major cottage industry. And well it should have been.
If developing countries in other regions were to experience the economic
growth that countries like Korea and Taiwan enjoyed from the 1960s to the
1990s, an enormous increase in levels of human welfare would result. Since
the end of 1997, collective obsession with 'what went wrong' has almost
put an end to efforts to understand an institutional context that produced 30
years of extraordinary growth. This is unfortunate, especially since 'what
went wrong' almost certainly includes deterioration of the generative
institutional context and diagnosing deterioration requires a clear
understanding of the original. This contribution assumes that the
institutional lessons of the original 'East Asian Miracle' are still worth
learning and tries to decipher what they might be.

Peter Evans, Department of Sociology, University of California, Berkeley.

Extracting the relevant elements of the institutional context and formulating them at a level of generality appropriate for possible transfer to societies with different cultures and histories is a formidable challenge. The first step is deciding what features of the multifaceted East Asian institutional context might constitute prerequisites for successful policy implementation. This, in turn, requires a characterisation of the successful policies themselves. There are currently at least three competing ways of characterising East Asian economic policies. They might be called the 'market-friendly model', the 'industrial policy model' and the 'profit-investment nexus model'.

The 'market-friendly model', exemplified by the World Bank's [1993] *East Asian Miracle* report, focuses on 'getting the fundamentals right'. Government must preserve macroeconomic stability and provide 'rules of the game' that are transparent and predictable. Economic bureaucracies must resist demands by business for market-distorting subsidies and protections while still retaining business confidence. This model requires public bureaucracies with general economic competence, but not bureaucrats with entrepreneurial flair or specific knowledge of industrial operations.

The 'industrial policy' model, epitomised by Johnson's classic [1982] study of MITI (Ministry of International Trade and Industry) and later refined in the works of Amsden [1989] and Wade [1990], demands more of the economic policy makers. In addition to providing the predictable, market-friendly, macroeconomic environment required by the first model, policy has an entrepreneurial function. Policies nurturing the general macroeconomic environment must be complemented by industry-specific policies that push sectors most worth pursuing and shift capital out of sectors with declining returns and weak growth prospects. The effective application of industry-specific incentives requires policies that 'discipline' business in the sense of making sure that a performance *quid pro quo* is delivered in return for subsidies.

The 'profit-investment nexus' model [*Akyüz and Gore, 1996*] shares with the 'industrial policy model' the idea that policy must do more than simply provide a facilitative macroeconomic environment, but is not as demanding of industry-specific policies. For the profit-investment model to work, policies must increase the overall level of investment. Sustaining expectations of high profit rates, through a combination of subsidies and selective protection against external competition is the first step. Making sure that profits are channelled into reinvestment rather than consumption or speculation is the necessary second step. The emphasis is not on the allocative efficiency gained by selecting particular industrial sectors but on the high overall rate of capital accumulation.

Despite the important differences between these three models, they share a robust core as far as institutional prerequisites are concerned. All three require an exceptionally capable state bureaucratic apparatus in order to work. All three require relations between government and business that are close but preserve the government's ability to act independently of business pressures.

Consensus on the importance of bureaucratic competence is clear. Even the 'market-friendly' model, which places the least emphasis on state capacity, still demands a very high level of bureaucratic capability. Bureaucrats must have the technical competence to assess the potential effects of their policies, but technically accurate prediction of how rational entrepreneurs should respond to policies is only the first step. The economic bureaucracy as a whole must be sufficiently coherent so that policies do not work at cross-purposes. Equally important, economic bureaucracies must generate sufficient confidence in the minds of the always sceptical audience of private entrepreneurs so that they are willing to bet their capital in ways that will make expected policy outcomes a reality. Putting all of this together is a tall order.

The industrial policy and profit-investment nexus models require even more capable bureaucracies. Knowledge and understanding of sectorally specific industrial operations are crucial to the industrial policy model, and aggressive public entrepreneurship is implied in both models. However, for purposes of thinking about institutional prerequisites, the emphasis on the importance of higher levels of bureaucratic capacity, which is shared by all three models, is a sufficient core. If developing countries in other regions could achieve the levels of bureaucratic capacity entailed in the 'market-friendly' model, the additional capacity implied by the other models would be institutionally within reach.

There is also a surprising degree of common ground across the three models with regard to the requisite business-government relations. None of the models is consistent with traditional images of ivory tower bureaucrats constructing policy on the basis of abstract rules applied in isolation from entrepreneurial elites. All three agree on the importance of close ties across the public-private divide. Close ties are the *sine qua non* of being able to maintain credibility over time in spite of the policy failures and reversals which must inevitably afflict even the most capable policy makers. From the point of view of the market-friendly model, close ties are also necessary in order to insure accountability. Bureaucrats need to understand the needs and interests of business in order to be effectively market-friendly. The industrial policy model implies much denser and more intimate ties, since bureaucrats must have access to information about industrial operations at the sectoral level.

All three models are equally adamant on the importance of avoiding capture. Adherents of the market-friendly model are clearly conscious of the dangers of regulations being shaped to serve the needs of particular businesses. The problem of capture is even more important to the industrial policy and profit-investment nexus models precisely because the creation of rents is so central to the process of accumulation in both these models. If rents are created without the enforcement of a developmental quid pro quo from entrepreneurs, the strategy will have perverse effects. As UNCTAD [*1996: 13*] puts it: 'Not only does the creation of rents mean a sacrifice in current income and the transfer of resources to activities with more uncertain prospects, but there is real danger that these rents, unless skilfully managed, can become permanent, weakening entrepreneurship and hampering productivity growth in the long run.'

In my own work [*Evans, 1995*], I have called this apparently contradictory combination of close ties and independence that is central to all three models 'embedded autonomy'. I have also emphasised that the possibility of sustaining this apparently paradoxical form of government-business relations is contingent on preserving the internal cohesion and coherence of state bureaucracies. The requisite pattern of government-business relations cannot be separated from the institutional character of the bureaucracies themselves.

In sum, agreement on basic institutional prerequisites transcends continuing disagreements over which facets of policy are most crucial to East Asia's economic success. Across various interpretations of policy there is shared conviction that economic success requires a highly capable, coherent economic bureaucracy, closely connected to but still independent of the business community. If there are transferable lessons to be gained from East Asia's success, they almost certainly begin with this institutional combination.

It may, of course, be argued that the ability to construct analogues to these proximate institutional prerequisites is in turn contingent on the broader social structural context. A relatively low level of inequality, particularly as regards agricultural landholdings is the most obvious candidate. Most analysts agree that the egalitarian character of East Asian growth is one of its most important distinctive features. Some, like Campos and Root [*1996*] consider it 'the key to the Asian miracle'. Likewise, it may be argued that East Asian economic transformation involved the intersection of national institutions with a particular configuration of global institutions. Most would agree that the 'post-WTO' (World Trade Organisation) global context is different from the one in which the East Asian countries succeeded in transforming themselves into industrial powers.

If economic bureaucracies and government-business relations analogous to those that prevailed in East Asia seem constructible in principle, then broader contextual issues like social structural preconditions and the 'post-WTO' global environment take on greater importance. On the other hand, if even the proximate institutional prerequisites seem beyond the reach of developing countries in other regions, then whether or not they could be initiated in less egalitarian settings and in a twenty-first century global context is a moot point. It makes sense, therefore, to first explore the transferability of proximate institutional prerequisites and then return to contextual questions.

A more accurate sense of what is meant by 'capable, coherent economic bureaucracies' and 'embedded autonomy' requires a better picture of the way in which these institutions manifested themselves in various East Asian countries during the period of their industrial transformation. I will take Japan, Korea and Taiwan as the exemplars of East Asian institutional forms (adding a few side glances at Singapore). First, I will review briefly some of the features of economic bureaucracies in these countries. Then I will examine patterns of government/business relations, focusing on the evolution of these relations over time. With this grounding, I will return in the conclusion to the basic issue of whether proximate institutional prerequisites appear, in principle, to be constructible in other social structural contexts under contemporary global conditions.

I. EAST ASIAN ECONOMIC BUREAUCRACIES

Nearly everyone agrees that when East Asian public bureaucracies are compared with those of developing countries in other regions they more closely approximate the ideal typical 'Weberian bureaucracy' [cf. Evans, 1995; Evans and Rauch, 1997; Rauch and Evans, 1997]. Meritocratic recruitment to public service and public service careers offering long-term rewards commensurate with those obtainable in the private sector were institutional cornerstones of the East Asian economic miracle. Nonetheless, exaggerated projections of East Asian bureaucracies as unalloyed repositories of competence and virtue seriously distort the lessons of the East Asian experience.

Without in any way undercutting the role of bureaucratic capability and cohesion in the East Asia cases, three points need to be underlined. First, there is not a single East Asian pattern. Even when we limit discussion to Japan, Korea, Taiwan and Singapore, the East Asia cases constitute a collective monument to the range of different concrete forms which bureaucratic organisation can take without losing the essential features necessary for effective performance. Second, as many authors, including

Cheng, Haggard and Kang [*1995*], have stressed, public bureaucracies capable of fostering effective economic performance in global markets were not some kind of natural resource, immediately available to East Asia following the Second World War. Modern East Asian bureaucracies were constructed through intense, prolonged struggles for reform and endless experimentation over the course of the post-Second World War period. Third, East Asian bureaucracies are not only different across countries. Their character also varies substantially across agencies within countries. While some agencies may look very much like the Weberian ideal, others have the kind of clientelistic character that is normally associated with Latin America.

Variation across countries can be nicely illustrated by looking at methods of recruitment. Japan and Korea both have very powerful exam-based systems of recruitment. During most of the post-Second World War period, passing the higher civil service examination has been the goal of tens of thousands of graduates from elite universities. Since only about two per cent of those who take the exam pass, the civil service has had its pick among the 'best and the brightest' and those who pass the exam enjoy tremendous prestige and commensurate *esprit de corps*.[1] Singapore's system is quite different.[2] There is no unified civil service exam along Japanese or Korea lines. Instead, the 'best and the brightest' are identified based on their performance in secondary school and given government scholarships for higher education in return for a commitment to enter the civil service, provided, of course, that they continue to perform at the top of their cohorts. Taiwan represents a third variation. The higher civil service exam is used as a filter for many parts of the bureaucracy, but key economic and planning agencies rely on the meritocratic selectivity of Taiwan National University plus successful completion of graduate training abroad [*Cheng et al., 1995*]. In short, meritocratic recruitment can be achieved through a variety of means.

In order to be effective, meritocratic recruitment must be complemented by a career structure that produces rewards commensurate with those that capable individuals could attain in the private sector. Salaries do not necessarily have to be equal, but the combination of salary, intrinsic job satisfaction, perquisites, security and prestige has to be close enough to the combination of rewards available in the private sector to ensure that public managers are as capable as private ones. Here again there is variation. All of the East Asian countries pay bureaucrats much more generously than do most developing countries, but Singapore is exceptional in its efforts to keep public salaries at or above private levels. Bureaucratic salaries in Korea and Taiwan tend to be only about two thirds of private salaries, but the gap is closed in other ways.[3] In Korea, a complex system of allowances complements salaries [*Campos and Root, 1996: 146*]. In Taiwan, key economic agencies are kept outside and substantially above the regular civil service scales.[4] The important point is that, despite having different strategies, all of these countries operate on the assumption that keeping rewards in the public and private sectors commensurate is the goal.[5]

Having a cohesive collection of capable individuals does not ensure coherent public action. Effective state policy also requires a structure that resolves issues of jurisdiction and coordination. As Wade [*1990*] points out, East Asian industrial policies are typically built around a 'pilot agency' that shapes development initiatives, (for example, the Economic Planning Board in Korea, the Council on Economic Planning and Development in Taiwan, MITI in Japan, the Economic Planning Board in Singapore). Still, there is wide variation in the overall organisation of East Asian economic bureaucracies. In Japan and Korea, line ministries (Finance and Industry) tended to hold sway. On the other hand, as Cheng *et al.* emphasise, Taiwan relied very heavily during the formative period of its industrialisation process on a shifting variety of 'task forces' that were outside of the formal ministerial structure. Coherence was achieved by the strong continuity in the economic technocrats who shifted positions but maintained a vision of the overall developmental enterprise. In Singapore, while the EPB and the Ministry of Finance provide a general vision, a great deal of the state action is executed by an array of statutory boards, each independent and specialised with full responsibility for accomplishing a particular task (for example, the Housing Development Board). Once again, it is not that there is a single organisational formula that other developing countries must replicate. Instead, there are a variety of ways to create a coherent bureaucracy. Would-be borrowers have a great deal of room for creative flexibility in trying to build locally viable equivalents.

One of the greatest dangers in *post hoc* efforts to draw lessons from East Asian economic bureaucracies is to assume that they have either always been there or somehow emerged effortlessly out of more traditional pre-Second World War governmental organisations. As everyone who has studied East Asian bureaucracies in depth is careful to point out (for example, Amsden, Johnson, Wade, etc.), this is hardly the case. Building these bureaucracies was a hard fought struggle whose outcome was often in doubt. The struggle against corrosion from corruption has been a continual effort of equal intensity. East Asian bureaucracies are neither gifts from the past nor easy outgrowths of surrounding social organisation. They are hard won edifices constantly under reconstruction.[6]

Taiwan is an obvious case in point. Arriving on Taipei with the knowledge that it must either reinvent itself or disappear, the Guomindang revamped its central administrative structures (for example cutting the number of ministries in half) and set up a 'Control Yuan' powerful enough to impeach even Chiang Kai-shek's nephew [*Root, 1996: 34, 37*]. The struggle to construct an effective public bureaucracy in Korea was no less intense. Under Syngman Rhee, civil service exam results were ignored in filling over 95 per cent of the higher civil service positions. In this period Korea was sending its bureaucrats to Pakistan to learn economic policy-making [*UNCTAD, 1996: 28*] and U.S. advisors despaired of ever creating a meritocratic bureaucracy. When Park Chung Hee and his reform-bent fellow junior officers took over in 1961, they dismissed more than 35,000 civil servants and began reconstruction from the ground up [*Cheng et al., 1995: 52–3*]. Despite continual efforts at reconstruction, corruption, of course, remains a central concern in all East Asian countries.8 The lesson to be drawn from the East Asian experience is not that pervasive rectitude is a precondition for effective state action; it is that even imperfect governmental machinery, operating with normally venal human beings, can still be moulded into an instrument capable of facilitating high rates of economic growth.

This point must be made even more strongly if the focus is expanded from key economic agencies to the bureaucracy as a whole. With the possible exception of Singapore, all of these bureaucracies contain large 'pockets of conspicuous inefficiency' [*Okimoto, 1989: 4*]. In Japan, agriculture and construction are clientelistic contrasts to MITI and the Ministry of Finance. In Korea, Cheng et al. [*1995: 49*] describe Park Chung Hee as having 'bifurcated' the bureaucracy, leaving ministries like construction to satisfy clientelistic needs while he focused reform efforts on the key economic ministries. Cheng et al. also point out [*1995: 44*] that while the KMT (Guomindang) was careful to keep access to key economic agencies strictly meritocratic, other parts of the civil service were less well protected. Meritocratic recruitment rules were diluted by 'backdoor' examinations to funnel KMT Party elites and retired military officers into state bureaucracies and special provincial quotas for descendants of mainlanders. Overall bureaucratic effectiveness does not require that state bureaucracies are uniformly exemplary. A substantial share of the benefits of superior bureaucratic performance may be obtained by focusing reforms on a relatively small set of key economic agencies.

What this review suggests is that the challenge of emulating East Asia's bureaucratic effectiveness may be less daunting than the stereotypical 'Confucian super-bureaucrat' image might suggest. Meritocracy and organisational coherence can be secured though in a variety of institutional forms. Most countries should be able to find one suited to local history and politics. Uniformly exemplary bureaucracies are not necessary, only selectively exemplary ones. Construction of such bureaucracies was difficult in East Asia and will be difficult elsewhere, but there is no obvious reason to believe that it is beyond reach.

II. GOVERNMENT–BUSINESS RELATIONS

Given a capable, internally coherent state bureaucracy, the next challenge is connecting bureaucrats and corporations. In East Asia the connection was made on at least two different levels. On the most general level, East Asian governments managed to diffuse a sense that they were genuinely committed a collective project of national development. Despite political divisions and governmental missteps, this sense of a national project gained surprisingly widespread credence and constituted one of the most important 'collective goods' provided by the state. The essential complement to this broad ideological connection was a dense set of concrete interpersonal ties that enabled specific agencies and enterprises to construct joint projects at the sectoral level. Like the bureaucracy itself, neither kind of connection sprang into place full blown at the end of the Second World War. The evolution of government-business ties in East Asia has been even more convoluted and counter intuitive than the evolution of the bureaucracy itself.

Some portrayals of contemporary East Asian government-business relations, such as the Bank's *East Asian Miracle* report, give the impression of bland, tension-free consensus. More historically oriented analyses (such as Cheng *et al.*) give a different picture. Deep scepticism with regard to the potential developmental contribution of the local business community was fundamental to the early phases of government-business relations in both Taiwan and Korea. Neither regime assumed that the pursuit of profit would naturally lead local entrepreneurs to make transformative investments. Instead, local businesses were perceived as 'rent seekers' who were looking for officially sanctioned niches that would allow them to buy cheap and sell dear without having to risk entry into newer, more challenging sectors. Nor was this perception unjustified. In the 1950s the heads of the Korean *chaebol* did not behave like Schumpeterian industrialists willing to risk hundreds of millions of dollars in order to get into high return, high growth sectors. At best, they were crafty traders, exploiting the privilege of importing simple consumer goods, like sugar, flour and cotton, to make a killing on the domestic market. The business groups that had surrounded the KMT on the mainland were of the same ilk. Given this, it is not surprising that there was such a strong faction in the KMT that favoured using state-owned as the primary instrument of the country's industrialisation. Nor is it surprising the Park Chung Hee and his radical young officers paraded businessmen through the streets in dunce caps.

Being sceptical of the developmental contribution of local business groups was rational, but learning to work with them was a necessity. Even Park Chung Hee, probably the most ideologically anti-business of East Asia's industrialising leaders, soon decided that industrial transformation would require enlisting the services of the *chaebol*. Enlisting business leaders also meant sanctioning the expansion of private economic power, something that political leaders in other regions have often been loath to allow.

Openness to the growth of private power was made more likely by two things. First came the conviction that industrialisation was the *sine qua non* of regime survival. Maintaining political dominion by monopolising control over a stagnant economy did not look like a viable option in the geopolitical environment of post-Second World War East Asia. East Asia's political leadership made a long term bet that economic transformation was the best means of maintaining political power. The willingness to do so depended in turn on confidence that the state apparatuses they commanded were sufficiently robust to survive a process of industrial transformation that would inevitably shift more power (political as well as economic) to private corporations. In short, confidence in the state's capacity was a precondition for willingness to accept the growth of private power.

The decision to enlist private capital did not erase scepticism. Rather it was the synthesis of scepticism and enlistment that formed the heart of East Asian government-business relations. Commitment to collaborating with private corporations never meant taking it for granted that local business groups would behave like Schumpeterian entrepreneurs. Instead, transforming the character of private corporate elites was assumed to be an essential part of the development strategy. The general philosophy of engagement and support coupled with scepticism and pressure translated concretely into policies of rent creation plus discipline, policies which proved eminently successful in the transformation of corporate behaviour. Established firms like Samsung were moved from unrelieved concentration on commercial rents to regular forays into genuinely Schumpeterian risk-taking (as in semiconductors) while new firms, like Taiwan's ACER, were nurtured from small scale manufacturing success to world-wide competitive presence in 'hi-tech' sectors.

In Taiwan and Korea, local firms were the primary targets of the support/performance bargain. Singapore showed that, given sufficient will and state capacity, the strategy could even be applied when corporate capital was primarily transnational. Over the course of the 1970s and 1980s Singapore's economic planners managed to convince TNCs to see the island not as an export processing zone for low wage, labour-intensive manufacturing but as an investment site for a combination of advanced high value-added manufacturing and information/service activities.

The 'support/performance bargain' could never have been implemented without a foundation of concrete interaction between economic bureaucrats and corporate managers. Effective government business relations depended on large volumes of high quality information flowing between government and corporations and on mutual confidence that predictions and commitments were credible. Neither could be generated by exchanging position papers and publicity releases. The 'embeddedness' of East Asian states was built on a concatenation of concrete ties at various levels, ranging from Park Chung Hee presiding over monthly export promotion meetings with the leaders of the *chaebol* to Industrial Development Bureau officials giving technical advice to small firms in Taiwan [*Wade, 1990*]. These networks were invaluable in generating business confidence, in overcoming coordination problems, in persuading firms to take bigger risks, and in giving the bureaucracy a realistic sense of whether or not its initiatives would be validated by corporate action.

Just as the concrete organisational structure of state bureaucracies varied substantially from country to country, so did the concrete organisation of government-business ties. Japan's 'deliberation councils' are the archetype. Organised and staffed by the state (in this case MITI), they provide a forum for private entrepreneurs to filter to policy proposals. What does not fly in a deliberation council is unlikely to work in practice. Conversely, when proposals succeed in generating the support of deliberation councils, MITI can be confident that the appropriate private sector response will be forthcoming. Korea used a similar procedure to coordinate its export promotion drive and insure that the connection between subsidies and export performance was clearly communicated.

In Taiwan, the KMT's reluctance to include Taiwanese business leaders in the mainlander-dominated process of policy formation made deliberation councils an uncomfortable form. Alternative forms emerged. In cases where the government agency seemed to be really going astray, the KMT's response was to create 'a task force led and managed by the private sector to perform the functions of the ailing agency or bureau' [*Campos and Root, 1996: 119*]. During the late 1970s and early 1980s, periodic large-scale conferences, which brought together major business leaders along with academics and government technocrats gave economic policy-makers an opportunity to gauge the likely response to new policy initiatives.[8] By the end of the 1980s, relations between the KMT and local business had progressed to the point that an Industrial Development Consultative Council, modelled on the Japanese deliberation councils was introduced, albeit with a smaller proportion of business representation than in the Japanese case.[9] In Singapore, the fact that the crucial private actors are largely transnational makes a Taiwanese-style 'conference' format easier than deliberation councils, and the Economic Development Bureau (EDB) has made good use of this format.[10] As in the organisation of the bureaucracy itself, there are multiple routes to building effective government–business ties.

Government–business ties are as important at the level of implementation as they are in policy formation. Relationships between agencies and individual firms can expand the information available to firms about technological 'best practice' and foreign markets, overcome coordination problems, and lower the perceived risks to entrepreneurial initiatives. The impact of such networks has been particularly important in pushing East Asian firms to move into more technologically challenging sectors. Both the economic bureaucracy and state-owned firms have played important roles.

The role of the Japanese state in generating one of the world's most powerful information technology sectors is a classic case. From the early relationships between Japan's state-owned Nippon Telephone and Telegraph (NTT) and its suppliers, through MITI's creation of the Japan Electronic Computer Corporation (JECC) to ease the cash flow problems of local computer producers, to the various MITI-sponsored collaborative research projects on semi-conductors, close working relationships between state agencies and individual firms were an essential part of turning Japanese corporations into global players in the information technology sector.[11]

Dense government-business ties focused on enhancing the competitiveness of individual firms have been equally important in the emergence of more technologically advanced industries in Korea and Taiwan. In Korea, for example, the Electronics and Telecommunications Research Institute (ETRI), an offshoot of the Ministry of Communications, played a 'MITI-like' catalytic role in pushing the pace at which the *chaebol* moved forward in semiconductor technology by organising a series of collaborative research and development projects. Only relatively small amounts of subsidised finance involved in these projects, but they signalled that MOC considered this an important area for firms to be involved, made each of the *chaebol* aware of the progress the others were making and raised the perceived cost of lagging behind [*Evans, 1995: 141*]. In Taiwan, the Electronics Research and Service Organisation (ERSO) played a similar role in helping small computer producers develop their own personal computer designs by means of MITI-like collaborative research consortia.[12] Again Singapore offers an interesting variation on the theme. At the end of the 1980s, local members of the Singapore Manufacturers Association expressed interest in Batam industrial park that was proposed as part of the

EDB's 'Riau–Johor–Singapore Growth Triangle'. In order to get them to move ahead, however, it took major concrete commitments to the project on the part of the state-owned Singapore Technologies Industrial Corporation (whose Chairman was conveniently also Chair of the EDB at the time) [*Koh, 1995: 428-31*].

The synthesis of scepticism and enlistment has proved its effectiveness in East Asia, but the system's very success makes it hard to perpetuate. The very growth transformation of local corporations that past patterns of government–business relations have fostered has created a local entrepreneurial class much less amenable to being prodded by the state. Among the *chaebol* there were none whose growth was more entwined with government policy than Hyundai, yet when Chung Ju Yung, Hyundai's founder, ran for President in 1992, his slogan was 'Get government out of business' [*Evans, 1995: 229*].

This example serves to illustrate what is logically obvious. When the 'East Asia miracles' began, local business was weak, depending on the state for both capital and protection from international competition. The definition of successful industrialisation is the creation of firms that can compete on international markets, both product markets and capital markets. Once they have achieved a measure of international competitiveness, the constraining effects of being tied into a national development project become more salient to local firms and the supportive benefits of national projects become less necessary. In short, East Asian government–business relations cannot be taken as a mechanical model which, once installed, inexorably grinds out the same economic results. Relations between the state and private capital have been in flux throughout the process of industrial transformation. Making sure that government-business relations continue to contribute to economic growth, like maintaining the calibre of the bureaucracy itself, will require constant, contentious effort combined with unflagging creativity, in East Asia as in other regions.

III. TRANSFERABLE LESSONS?

If transfer were defined literally as the implantation of replicas of East Asian institutions in developing countries of other regions, then it would make no sense. The concrete institutional forms associated with East Asian success vary substantially across individual countries for good reason. Achieving analytically similar results in different historical, cultural and political contexts requires adaptive 'reverse engineering'. Policies may be sometimes be transferable in the mechanistic sense of replication, but institutions rarely are. Individual East Asia countries discovered multiple specific routes to industrial transformation whose analytical commonalities hardly seemed evident while the process of institutional construction was under way. Other countries will have to use East Asian models as creatively as East Asians used the models that their American advisors presented them with in the 1950s.

Once the idea of transferable lessons is understood as an invitation to indigenous innovation that takes advantage of the underlying analytical logic of East Asian institutions, the possibility of exploiting of the East Asian experience becomes thoroughly plausible. If the reading of institutional prerequisites that I have presented here is reasonable, then constructing analytically analogous institutional forms in other countries is not a task beyond reach. Renovating institutional frameworks always requires political will, imagination and some luck, but the renovations implied by this analysis of East Asian institutions are no more daunting than those implied by admonitions to replicate an American style of market capitalism.

Building more effective public bureaucracies is obviously the first challenge. Earlier readings of East Asian success sometimes seemed to imply that what was required was a set of incorruptible super-bureaucrats able to out-manage professional managers and direct the operations of the private sector from a distance. This is almost certainly not the case. Brilliance never hurts, but motivated incumbents, whose level of competence is comparable to their private sector counterparts and who can have confidence in their peers, their organisations and their goals, are the core of an effective economic bureaucracy.

The lesson from East Asia is not that other developing countries must be able to count on impeccable bureaucracies in order to move forward, it is rather than they must be willing to invest resources, both political and economic, in the construction of a capable state apparatus. A clear commitment to reforming the bureaucracy, and a willingness to devote continual effort to preserving its competence lay at the root of East Asia's success.

The other important revision of the 'myth of the super-bureaucracy' is that renovation does not necessarily have to permeate the entire state apparatus. A few 'islands of efficiency' in the midst of a 'sea of clientelism' are not enough; they are too prone to being swamped by political waves. Minimal norms of probity and competence need to be applied on a general basis, but East Asian reformers did not attempt to transform every ministry. Radical changes were reserved for key economic agencies; routinized behaviour and surprisingly high levels of clientelism were allowed to persist in those considered less crucial to the national development project. Replicating East Asian bureaucratic success does not require a full renovation the state apparatus, only those parts of it most critical to effective economic policy-making.

Given this more realistic goal, the state bureaucracies of other developing countries appear less hopeless. Even with a more realistic sense of the institutional target, the magnitude of the task involved in building such bureaucracies should not be underestimated. Confronting vested interests, disrupting established repertoires and changing prevailing norms is never easy. None the less, existing public bureaucracies, certainly in Latin America and even to some degree in Africa, are not the irredeemable cesspools of incompetence that they are sometimes painted by neoliberal rhetoric. There are dedicated individuals working in public service in almost all countries. More important, most state bureaucracies, at least in Latin America, contain key agencies that at least in certain periods have displayed many of the institutional traits of 'Weberian bureaucracies'. Such agencies have performed with levels of efficacy comparable to those their East Asian counterparts, despite being surrounded by a public sector that is much less effectual overall. Almost every country has something to build on. The foundations may be less solid and extensive than they were in post-Second World War East Asia, but the challenge of building on them is more like the challenge faced by East Asian regimes than most readings of regional contrasts tend to admit.

Renovating state bureaucracies would make it qualitatively easier for other developing countries to generate more effective business-government relations. Still, the challenge of constructing a relationship in which a developmental quid pro quo is forthcoming from private elites in return for government support is even more daunting than the challenge of bureaucratic reform. In countries where governments have traditionally collaborated with private elites, as in Latin America, elites have usually extracted support without delivering. In countries where the development of private elites is historically shallow, as in Africa, public officials have usually been unwilling to construct a developmental bargain with local business apparently out of fear that the growth produced by such a bargain would threaten their own political control.

The possibility of breaking out of such ingrained patterns may depend on the larger context in which government-business relations are inserted, which brings us back to the two contextual issues mentioned at the beginning of this study. Are the capable, coherent state apparatuses and the combination of scepticism and rapprochement that characterises government-business relations in East Asia possible in the absence of the unusually egalitarian social structures that characterised East Asian countries after their post-Second World War land reforms? Does the more stringent, the 'post-WTO' world with its more intense internationalisation of business and more aggressive enforcement of neoliberal economic norms rob developing countries of the ability to offer local businesses the kind of support which forms the public side of the developmental bargain, leaving the private sector no reason to commit itself to the kind of aggressive reinvestment that constitutes its side of the bargain? If both these arguments are accepted in their strongest form, East Asian strategies are outside the institutional boundaries that other developing countries can hope to explore. I would argue, however, that, just as the barriers to constructing the proximate institutional prerequisites of East Asian economic policies are often exaggerated, the obstacles created by differences in social structural and geopolitical context are overstated as well.

The new global regulatory environment and the more highly internationalised structure of business organisation do make some of the policies used by the East Asian NICs more difficult to implement, but what puts East Asian practices out of reach is less likely to be external compulsion than anticipatory acquiescence by developing country governments to perceived constraints. Governments that persevere are likely to find ways of circumventing the new constraints. UNCTAD is almost certainly right when it argues [*1996: 39*] that, 'while the WTO multilateral agreements have reduced the scope of policy options, policy measures comparable to those applied by the East Asian countries can still be applied'.

The least developed countries are still free to offer a range of subsidies, other developing countries may have to become more subtle, but this is not inconsistent with following East Asian patterns. A substantial part of East Asian government–business relations have always been based in building credibility across the public–private divide through the regular exchange of information. Signalling and solving coordination problems among firms have played an important part in steering investments, perhaps as important as the subsidies themselves. Discipline of the private sector has often involved very conventional tools such as zealous income tax audits. None of this is placed out of bounds by the new international context. The argument might even be taken further: if new rules and climate stimulate the replacement of more heavy-handed versions of industrial policy with more sophisticated measures the current context could even end up making it easier for would-be emulators to stay on track in their efforts to transfer East Asian lessons. The rapid transformation of Singapore's industrialisation strategy offers a nice example of how 'industrial policy' can evolve in more sophisticated directions without losing any of its vitality.[13]

The problem of domestic social structural context may be more difficult to surmount. To begin with, gross inequality that is patently entrenched is a strong disincentive for the majority of the population to be 'future-oriented' and invest in their own human capital. But, the argument is not so much that inequality *per se* is a barrier to accumulation in economic terms. A concentration of returns on (reinvested) profits rather than wages should even help stimulate growth [cf. *You, 1996*]. The principal problem with inequality (beyond its negative welfare implications) is that it has corrosive institutional effect. Concentrated wealth and income generate concentrated private power, which in turn increases the likelihood that public institutions will be captured by private elites. At the same time entrenched inequality undercuts the legitimacy of state autonomy. As Campos and Root [*1996*] argue, the persistence of extreme levels of inequality makes it very hard for governments to credibly claim that they represent a national development project. When the absolute gap between rich and poor is growing, as in Latin America, populist clientelism seems to offer at least temporary relief to the excluded and close government-business ties look more like a conspiracy for redistribution upwards than a joint project of national development. Such domestic social structures more likely to be a barrier to renovating bureaucracies and building an effective government–business relations than the new international context.

The problem of domestic inequality forms the strongest basis for a pessimistic reading of the prospects of would-be emulators of East Asia success. Such a pessimistic reading starts from recognition that the initial societal conditions in East Asia, which underlay the proximate institutional prerequisites of successful policy, depended on a unique set of historical circumstances. The aftermath of the Second World War wiped out traditional elites, forced egalitarian reforms in agriculture, gave governments extraordinary leverage to reshape the behaviour of industrial elites and led these same governments to see their political survival as depending on rapid industrial growth. Equivalent surrounding conditions will not be replicated in Africa or Latin America in the foreseeable future. A more aggressively enforced internationalisation of the global economy, built around rules that work primarily to the benefit of current holders of financial capital and intellectual property, exacerbates the problem by encouraging passive conformity to corporate preferences. In this pessimistic reading, most citizens of Africa and Latin America are condemned to marginalisation within their domestic economies and exclusion from the fruits of growing global productivity.

Plausible as this pessimistic reading may be, there is no reason to consider it inevitable. To begin with, the mechanisms connecting initial levels of inequality and policy possibilities are much too subtle to justify giving up on the possibility of other Third World countries taking advantage of East Asian lessons simply on the basis of crude estimates of their size distribution of income.[14] (Malaysia and Singapore have been quite successful despite income size distributions substantially worse than all of South Asia and a good part of Africa.) Furthermore, if we agree that more inegalitarian social structures create obstacles to growth primarily because they afford particularistic private interests too much leverage and undercut the foundations of the scepticism/support/quid pro quo model of government–business relations that prevailed in East Asia, then the post-WTO world may in fact have some advantages. The new rules do give would-be industrialising regimes some leverage in resisting capture. They can claim, for example, 'our hands are tied by international rules' when non-performing corporations claim subsidies.[15] Likewise, externally enforced neoliberal reductions of state personnel, like any primitive slash and burn strategy of husbandry, at least creates some clear ground on which, in principle, stronger more capable government institutions could be built. Finally, the fact that the 'post-WTO' world forces a more global economic orientation has institutional advantages as well as disadvantages. Being able to define local welfare as depending on successful confrontation with an uncontrollable external environment is one of the best ways of legitimating the idea of a national development project.

Resisting fatalism is the first essential step in making the pessimistic scenario less plausible, especially in Africa and Latin America, where the disillusionment with prior national development strategies has left policy-makers (and their political constituents) with little confidence in their ability to create more effective institutions. Passive resignation to being positioned at the bottom of the hierarchy of nations is a self-fulfilling prophecy. Trying to transfer lessons from East Asia makes more sense. Constructing local counterparts to the proximate institutional prerequisites of East Asian success – bureaucracies with a capable economic core and government–business relations based on scepticism combined with communication and support in return for performance delivered – is not an impossible task.

Taking on the current global environment in the same way that East Asian countries took on the local destruction and geopolitically hostile regional environment left behind by the world's most destructive global war – as a challenge to which they had to produce a national response in order to survive – is the most productive response to the difficulties created by the forced acceleration of internationalisation. In the best of all possible worlds, African and Latin American countries would follow the lessons generated by the East Asian experience in the same way that East Asian policy-makers followed western models of capitalism: with such originality and inventiveness as to outperform the original. Hopefully the art of leapfrogging is not yet dead.

NOTES

1. This discussion draws heavily on Cheng, Haggard and Kang. For descriptions of the Japanese and Korean bureaucratic recruitment see also Johnson [1982], B.K. Kim [1987], Campos and Root [1996] and Root [1996].
2. Singapore's bureaucracy has been analysed in great depth by Jonathan Quah [e.g. 1982, 1984, 1993]. See also Gillian Koh's very extensive study [1995], as well as Campos and Root [1996], and Root [1996].
3. According to World Bank data, Singaporean public sector salaries are 114 per cent of comparable private sector salaries [World Bank, 1993: 187]. Even discounting the Singapore case, the contrast between East Asia, where salaries tend to run at two-thirds of private salaries in Latin America and other developing countries in Latin America and Africa where the ratio is closer to a quarter is striking. See Campos and Root [1996: 144].
4. According to Cheng, Haggard and Kang [1995: 45] pay in these elite agencies was five times higher than normal civil service pay in the 1950s and 50 per cent higher in the 1970s.
5. In a number of countries regular surveys to make sure salaries are not falling too far behind private salaries. For example, Japan's National Personnel Authority runs an extensive annual salary survey [Campos and Root, 1996: 145,] as does Hong Kong [Root, 1996: 56].
6. This is not to say that earlier, more traditional, bureaucratic forms did not provide important foundations. Confucian examination systems, British and Japanese colonial administrations and pre-Second World War efforts at economic development all offered elements to build on. The crucial point is that an objective observer, surveying these elements at the close of the Second World War, would not necessarily have found them any more promising than the foundations available elsewhere in the Third World.
7. Hong Kong and Singapore have also had to struggle to contain corruption. In Hong Kong, large scale corruption was only brought under control after the creation of the exceptionally powerful and effective Independent Commission Against Corruption (ICAC) in 1974 [Root, 1996: 57–8; Campos and Root, 1996: 169–70]. Singapore's Corrupt Practices Investigation Bureau (CPIB) was given equally extensive powers from the beginning of the island's history as an independent state.
8. See Cheng, Haggard and Kang [1995: 63–5] for a description of these conferences and a listing of dates and titles.
9. Cheng, Haggard and Kang report an initial proportion of only one sixth businessmen, whereas business leaders formed the majority of participants in the Japanese case [Campos and Root, 1996: 82–9].
10. See Koh [1995: 416–18] for a description of the 'Global Strategies' conferences organised by the EDB which brought together a thousand senior TNC executives for two days of sessions on Singapore's proposed economic policies at the end of the 1980s.
11. Flamm [1987] and Anchordoguy [1988] provide excellent descriptions of the organisation of government business ties during the emergence of Japan's information technology sector.
12. See Noble [1988]. Wade [1990] offers numerous other examples. See also Ernst and O'Connor [1992].
13. The Economic Development Board's revitalisation under Philip Yeo and Tan Chin Nam around a strategy aimed at 'marketing' Singapore to TNCs as a site for information and service intensive operational headquarters is an interesting case in point [cf. Koh, 1995: Ch.4].
14. You [1996] does a fine job of making it clear that, while the original East Asian success stories (Japan, Korea and Taiwan) are clearly unusual in their egalitarian distributions of wealth and income, the variations across different dimensions of distribution and the way in which they have changed over time are much too complex to be used as an argument for arbitrarily eliminating the possibility of other countries replicating East Asian institutional forms.
15. For a general discussion of the possibility of using international constraints as domestic leverage, see Evans, Jacobson and Putnam [1993].

REFERENCES

Akyüz, Yilmaz lmaz and Charles Gore, 1996, 'The Investment-Profits Nexus in East Asian Industrialisation', Background paper prepared for the Conference on 'East Asian Development: Lessons for a New Global Environment,' Kuala Lumpur, Malaysia, 29 Feb. and 1 March (see also published version in *World Development*, Vol.24, No.3).

Amsden, Alice, 1989, *Asia's Next Giant: South Korea and Late Industrialisation*, New York: Oxford University Press.

Anchordoguy, Marie, 1988, 'Mastering the Market: Japanese Government Targeting of the Computer Industry', *International Organisation*, Vol.42, No.3, pp.509–43.

Campos, Jose Egardo and Hilton L. Root, 1996, *The Key to the Asian Miracle: Making Shared Growth Credible*, Washington, DC: The Brookings Institution.

Cheng, Tun-jen, Stephan Haggard and David Kang, 1995, 'Institutions, Economic Policy and Growth in Korea and Taiwan', Paper presented at UNCTAD Seminar on 'Development of East and South-East Asia and a New Development Strategy – the Role of Government', 30–31 Oct. 1995, Geneva, Switzerland.

Ernst, Dieter and David O'Connor, 1992, *Competing in the Electronics Industry: The Experience of Newly Industrialising Countries* (an OECD Development Centre Study), Paris: OECD.

Evans, Peter, 1995, *Embedded Autonomy: States and Industrial Transformation*, Princeton, NJ: Princeton University Press.

Evans, Peter, Harold Jacobson and Robert Putnam (eds.), 1993, *Double-Edged Diplomacy: International Bargaining and Domestic Politics*, Berkeley, CA: University of California Press.

Evans, Peter and James Rauch, 1997, 'Bureaucracy and Growth: A Cross-National Analysis of the Effects of *Weberian* State Structures on Economic Growth', unpublished manuscript University of California, Berkeley, CA.

Flamm, Kenneth, 1987, *Targeting the Computer*, Washington, DC: The Brookings Institution.

Johnson, Chalmers, 1982, *MITI and the Japanese Miracle: the Growth of Industrial Policy, 1925-1975*, Stanford, CA: Stanford University Press.

Kim, Byung Kook, 1987, 'Bringing and Managing Socioeconomic Change: The State in Korea and Mexico', Ph.D. dissertation, Harvard University, Department of Government, Boston, MA.

Koh, Gillian, 1995, 'A Sociological Analysis of the Singapore Administrative Elite: The Bureaucracy in an Evolving Developmentalist State', Ph.D. Dissertation, University of Sheffield, Sheffield, UK.

Okimoto, Daniel I, 1989, *Between MITI and the Market: Japanese Industrial Policy for High Technology,* Stanford, CA: Stanford University Press.

Noble, Gregory, 1988, 'Between Cooperation and Competition: Collective Action in the Industrial Policy of Japan and Taiwan', Ph.D. dissertation, Harvard University, University Microfilms, Department of Government, Boston, MA.

Quah, Jonathan, 1982, 'The Public Bureaucracy and National Development in Singapore', in K.K. Tummala (ed.) *Administrative Systems Abroad*, Washington, DC: University Press of America.

Quah, Jonathan, 1984, 'The Public Policy Making Process in Singapore', *Asian Journal of Public Administration*, Vol.6, pp.108–26.

Quah, Jonathan, 1993, 'The Rediscovery of the Market and Public Administration: Some Lessons from the Singapore Experience', *Australian Journal of Public Administration*, Vol.52, No.3, pp.320–8.

Rauch, James and Peter Evans, 1997, 'Bureaucratic Structure and Bureaucratic Performance in Less Developed Countries', unpublished, University of California, San Diego.

Root, Hilton L., 1996, *Small Countries, Big Lessons: Governance and the Rise of East Asia* (published for the Asian Development Bank), Hong Kong: Oxford University Press.

UNCTAD (United Nations Conference on Trade and Development), Global Interdependence Division, 1996, 'Report to the Conference on East Asian Development: Lessons for a New Global Environment', Kuala Lumpur, Malaysia, 29 Feb. and 1 March.

Wade, Robert, 1990, *Governing the Market: Economic Theory and the Role of Government in*

Taiwan's Industrialisation, Princeton, NJ: Princeton University Press.

World Bank, 1993, *The East Asian Miracle: Economic Growth and Public Policy*, New York: Oxford University Press.

You, Jong-Il, 1996, 'Income Distribution and Growth in East Asia', Background paper for the UNCTAD *Trade and Development Report, 1996*, June.

Institutions and Growth in Korea and Taiwan: The Bureaucracy

TUN-JEN CHENG, STEPHAN HAGGARD and
DAVID KANG

*How do competent bureaucracies emerge in developing countries?
We examine bureaucratic reform in Korea and Taiwan and argue
that in both cases political leaders had an interest in reforming the
civil service to carry out their programmatic initiatives. In
addition, both governments undertook organisational reforms that
made certain parts of the bureaucracy more meritocratic, while
utilising centralised and insulated 'pilot agencies' in overall policy
coordination. However, we reject the approach to bureaucratic
reform that focuses primarily on its efficiency-enhancing effects. If
delegation, bureaucratic and policy reform provided an easily
available solution to the authoritarian's dilemma, dictators would
have more uniformly positive economic records. Rather, we analyse
the political and institutional constraints under which governing
elites operate. In doing so, we underscore several important
variations in the design of bureaucratic organisation, which in turn
mirror larger policy differences between the two countries.*

In the last decade, the debate about the role of government in the growth of
the East Asian newly industrialising countries (NICs) – Hong Kong, Korea,
Singapore and Taiwan – has undergone an evolution. The initial controversy
centred on the effects of economic policy. Neoclassical interpretations
emphasised the role of stable macroeconomic policy, outward-oriented
trade and exchange rate regimes, and market-conforming microeconomic
policies. Dissenters placed more weight on targeted industrial policies and

Tun-Jen Cheng, Department of Political Science, College of William and Mary, Williamsburg,
Virginia; Stephan Haggard, Graduate School of International Relations and Pacific Studies,
University of California, San Diego; David Kang, Government Department, Dartmouth College,
Hanover, New Hampshire.

on aggregate investment [*Amsden, 1989; Wade, 1990*].

Though this controversy continues, a second debate has arisen over the political and institutional foundations of rapid growth. To claim that policy mattered only pushed the puzzle of East Asia's growth back another step; policy choices themselves had to be explained. Analysis initially focused on the authoritarian, centralised, and insulated nature of political institutions in East Asia [*Johnson, 1982; Cheng, 1990; Gold, 1980, 1986; Gereffi and Wyman, 1990; Haggard, 1990*]. 'Strong' states had the political capability to respond flexibly to opportunities and to avoid the rent-seeking pressures that were typical of the policy-making process in other developing countries. As Alice Amsden [*1989*] put it succinctly, the capacity of the state to 'discipline' the private sector was an integral component of the East Asian miracle.

A correlate of this approach was an emphasis on the bureaucracy [*Johnson, 1982; Evans, 1992, 1995; Kang, 1997*]. Even champions of minimalist government could agree that a competent bureaucracy was important for effective economic policy; a well-organised and meritocratic bureaucracy was even more crucial for those who saw industrial policy as an integral element of the region's growth [*Chang, 1993*].

Yet the question of how competent bureaucracies emerge has received surprisingly little attention [*Geddes, 1994*]. Under what conditions do political leaders have an incentive to create such institutions, and why do they take the shape they do? Campos and Root [*1995, Ch.6*] offer an explanation that is rooted in a fundamental dilemma of authoritarianism, which until the 1980s was the characteristic form of political rule in most of the high-growth Asian countries. Dictators have difficulty convincing economic agents of the security of property rights and the stability of a given strategy because their powers allow them to change policy at will. One means of solving this problem is through delegation: to grant decision-making powers to relatively insulated technocratic agencies. Of course, if the dictator can delegate, he can also take authority back. However, he does so only at a cost. By raising the cost of reneging, delegation enhances the credibility of the government with economic agents.

We agree with Campos and Root that bureaucratic reform in Korea and Taiwan supported the broader policy projects of the authoritarian rulers, who initiated the two countries' export-led growth strategies: the Kuomintang (Nationalist) Party (KMT) in Taiwan and the military government under Park Chung Hee that came to power in Korea in 1961. In both cases, political leaders had an interest in reforming the civil service to carry out their programmatic initiatives. In both cases, governments undertook organisational reforms that improved the internal incentive structure and made the bureaucracy – or certain parts of it – more meritocratic. In both cases we find evidence that centralised and insulated 'pilot agencies' played a role in overall policy coordination.

However, we reject the approach to bureaucratic reform – or any policy change – that focuses primarily on its efficiency-enhancing effects. If delegation, bureaucratic and policy reform provided an easily available solution to the authoritarian's dilemma, dictators would have more uniformly positive economic records. Rather, we analyse the political and institutional constraints under which governing elites operate. In doing so, we underscore several important variations in the design of bureaucratic organisation, which in turn mirror larger policy differences between the two countries.

The existence of a dominant party organisation in Taiwan provided a degree of continuity in political organisation that was altogether lacking in Korea. A dominant party permitted much more extensive penetration of society, and substantially reduced opportunities for independent political and social organisation [*Gold, 1986*]. Because of political history, however, the KMT was more sensitive to inflation and rural interests than Korea's political leadership. Hyperinflation and failure to address the rural question were among the major reasons for the KMT's defeat by the Communist Party on the mainland. Bureaucratic organisation privileged policy in these areas through a strong rural reform commission and an independent Central Bank.

Second, and also in contrast to Korea, policy was initially biased to a much greater extent towards the state sector itself. The Kuomintang government, made up overwhelmingly of mainlanders, had few ties with the local Taiwanese private sector, nor any need for their political support. Conservatives in the party were highly suspicious of private economic power and favoured the maintenance of a substantial state-owned enterprise (SOE) sector. Bureaucratic organisation mirrored these priorities; the agencies providing direct support for the private sector were relatively weak and had few instruments when compared with their Korean counterparts.

Korea's politics has been substantially less stable than Taiwan's, oscillating between weak or highly controlled democracy and various forms of authoritarian rule. In Taiwan there was no fundamental change in regime until the political liberalisation of the 1980s, and that was initiated by the KMT leadership. In Korea, by contrast, we can distinguish at least eight distinct periods in the country's post-war political history: the nominally democratic government of Syngman Rhee (1948–60); the short-lived democratic Second Republic (1960–61); a period of outright military rule (1961–63); a return to a nominally democratic, but highly controlled democracy under Park Chung Hee (1964–72); a period of civilian authoritarian rule under the Yushin or 'revitalising' constitution (1973–79);

a brief political opening, following Park Chung Hee's assassination in 1979; a declaration of martial law and the continuation of authoritarian rule under Chun Doo Hwan's Fifth Republic (1980–87); and finally the transition to more fully democratic rule in 1987–88.

These broad political differences have had consequences for the organisation of the bureaucracy; we highlight two. First, the president has exercised greater direct control over policy-making in Korea, which has been much more centralised. Second, successive Korean governments have not had the same aversion to establishing close relations with the private sector. Under Syngman Rhee, these relations rested on substantial corruption and rent-seeking [*Haggard, Cooper and Moon, 1993*]. Park achieved his political aims *vis-à-vis* the private sector by strengthening the bureaucratic machinery that provided various forms of support to industry.

However, the very concentration that Korean industrial policy fostered ultimately served to undermine the authority of the technocrats. During the 1970s Park Chung Hee circumvented the economic bureaucracy altogether, a powerful reminder that if delegation can provide a partial solution to the authoritarian's dilemma it can never overcome it completely.

Since the policy reforms in the two countries have been amply described in the literature [*Krueger, 1979; Galenson, 1979*], we seek to focus attention on the less-studied phenomenon of the development of the bureaucracy in the two countries. We distinguish between the evolution of organisational structure and the management of personnel. First, how was the bureaucracy organised internally? To what extent was decision-making centralised? To what extent did particular agencies, such as the central bank or key planning agencies, enjoy autonomy from normal bureaucratic routine? Second, we examine the civil service itself: how economic bureaucrats were trained, recruited, promoted, compensated and overseen.

I. TAIWAN

One of the surprising features of the organisation of the economic bureaucracy in Taiwan is its fluidity. The organisational framework of economic planning has been remoulded numerous times during the post-war era, usually in line with internal political realignments. The result is a more fragmented structure than that visible in Korea. Economic policy jurisdictions have neither been concentrated nor hierarchically structured, with resulting fragmentation, parallel organisation and problems of coordination.

These apparent organisational problems have been partly overcome in two ways. First, concurrent appointments and distinctive personnel policies allowed particular individuals to serve coordinating roles [*Wade, 1990: 225;*

Haggard and Pang, 1994]. For example, in the 1950s, the heads of most economic ministries and agencies were concurrently members of two key bodies – the Economic Stabilisation Board (ESB) and the Council for US Aid (CUSA) – creating a structure that resembled interlocking corporate directorates. Patterns of promotion also facilitated coordination. Top bureaucrats are not generally recruited from outside the bureaucracy, but promoted from within; this has allowed a handful of the most important technocrats to establish relationships across a number of bureaus and to maintain continuity in the general direction of policy over time.

   A second mechanism of coordination arose from the fact that the early planning bodies and almost all major economic planning units – the ESB, CUSA, the Council on International Economic Cooperation and Development (CIECD), the Economic Planning Commission (EPC), and the Council on Economic Planning and Development (CEPD) – were constructed *outside* of the formal bureaucratic structure. This form of organisation was partly a response to the extraordinary situation in the early years of Taiwan's post-war development and partly a response to the need to maintain relations with the US aid machinery. These agencies were only gradually incorporated back into the bureaucracy over time, a task that was not fully completed until 1986.[1] Even as this process of gradual integration was taking place, the government continued to rely on the creation of specialised, small-scale units outside the normal ministerial structure in order to achieve particular objectives.

   The advantages of this organisational strategy were several. First, the structure contributed to agency independence. *Ad hoc* organs maintained direct links with the top political leadership, which gave key economic officials political backing and the ability to operate amid the confusion created by a large SOE sector, a complex national and provincial political structure, and the inertia of existing ministries [*Gold, 1986*]. The early post-aid period of the 1960s overlapped with a generational transition in the political leadership; poorly connected with the economic bureaucracy, Chiang Ching-kuo was much more hesitant than his father (Chiang Kai-shek) to grant discretion to the technocrats and took over the leadership of several key agencies himself. Nonetheless, the continued dominance of the presidency kept the economic bureaucracy insulated both from legislative scrutiny and from societal pressures more generally.

   The second advantage of this structure was that it allowed the government to bypass civil service regulations with respect to pay, and thus to attract the best people not only from the domestic labour pool but from the expatriate community as well. This parallel structure was facilitated by US aid, which encouraged the development of counterpart agencies.

   An important feature of the economic bureaucracy in Taiwan, when compared to Korea, is the relative standing of those agencies responsible for promoting industry. It is true that the economic planning agencies in Taiwan have controlled important policy instruments, including trade policy [*Wade, 1990: 224*]. However, it is also true that macroeconomic stability has been a central objective of the political leadership, and that both monetary and financial agencies were strongly insulated from the economic and industrial development agencies.

The Central Bank of China (CBC), restored in 1961, was until 1979 subordinated directly to the president. Its governor was appointed by the president for a term of five years without term limit and was accountable neither to the legislative branch nor to the premier or ministry of finance. Since 1979 the premier has nominated the governor of the CBC, but subject to final appointment by the president. As a member of the cabinet, the central bank governor attends cabinet meetings and can be called before the legislature for interpellation. However, unlike other cabinet members, the governor of the CBC serves for a fixed term; with the exception of one resignation due to health reasons, the governor has always served his or her entire term and in most cases has been reappointed.

The Ministry of Finance and the state-owned banks are also quite autonomous from the economic and industrial development agencies [*Cheng, 1993*]; there are few flows of personnel between these two domains and little ability on the part of the industry-oriented portions of the bureaucracy to direct the flow of resources from the state-owned banking system. This lack of financial instruments was not initially a handicap to industrial policy objectives because US aid was the major source not only of foreign exchange but of savings more generally. As aid fell off, however, and domestic savings became the major source of capital, the independence of state-owned banks necessarily diluted the ability of the economic planning agencies to pursue sector-specific policies. It was only after the Bank of Communication was rechartered as a development bank in 1979 that credit support and targeted lending became a tool of industrial policy.

Fiscal incentives remained the principal device for industrial promotion, but even the use of those instruments was hindered by the need to coordinate with the Ministry of Finance, which naturally had quite different incentives. These incentives were buttressed by the conservative macroeconomic policy preferences of the top political leadership and the fact that, with one exception, those premiers that have come from the economic bureaucracy have come from finance-related agencies rather than from the industrial development bureaucracy.

Organisational Structure

For the purpose of analysing the early development of the state apparatus, it is useful to divide the economic bureaucracy into three parts.[2] The first comprises the agencies for economic planning. A series of bureaucracies performed similar functions, yet held different hierarchical positions and power during different periods. Before the central government moved to Taiwan, it authorised the provincial government to create a liaison body, the Taiwan Production Board, to oversee the operations of the state enterprises that were relocated to Taiwan and the management and disposal of the properties inherited from the Japanese. It quickly assumed broader development planning functions. The Taiwan Production Board was absorbed into the Economic Stabilisation Board (ESB) in July 1953.[3] The ESB was chaired by the Governor of Taiwan, its members included the Ministers of Economic Affairs and Finance among others. The Board in turn had five divisions chaired by various ministers, but these divisions had no staff and served primarily a coordinating function.[4]

The first division of the ESB, however, was a key player in the evolution of early industrial policy in Taiwan, and played an important role in establishing relations with the Taiwanese private sector. An Industrial Development Commission (IDC) was established as a subsidiary of the first division to implement the industrial aspects of the first Four-Year Economic Development Plan (1953–56), which were drawn up by the ESB. The IDC had four sections – general industry, chemicals, transportation, and finance – and was staffed by over 30 full-time personnel. The IDC identified key projects and sought investors; it was after the formation of the IDC that the US aid agencies began to approve long-term investment projects [*Yen, 1989: 64,70; Kuo, 1995*].

A second organisational complex was the agencies for controlling foreign exchange and trade; in contrast to Korea, these were not closely integrated with industrial policy functions. To balance foreign trade and payments, an Industrial Finance Committee (IFC) was set up in June 1949 under the Taiwan Production Board. When this Board was merged into the Economic Stabilisation Board, however, the IFC was not moved; rather it was reorganised into an independent Foreign Exchange and Foreign Trade Committee, attached to the Taiwan provincial government and supervised by the Ministry of Economic Affairs and Ministry of Finance. In 1955, an independent Foreign Exchange and Trade Control Commission (FETCC) was established, which had a wide range of functions concerning the setting of the exchange rate, determining import requirements, screening foreign exchange applications and coordinating US aid, all of which gave it substantial power; again, these functions were separate from the planning activities of the ESB. The liberalising reforms of the late 1950s and early 1960s and the end of aid weakened the FETCC's clout, however; by the end of the decade, its trade functions had reverted to the Ministry of Economic

Affairs and the foreign exchange control function had been absorbed by the Central Bank [*Pang, 1992: 51–2*].

A final institutional complex was the agency for administering US aid, which gradually evolved into the country's core planning institutions in the 1960s. The CUSA began operations in 1950. The functions of the CUSA included the selection of aid projects, oversight of the local currency or counterpart programme, and maintaining a liaison with the US aid mission. When the ESB was dissolved in 1958, the CUSA proved the major bureaucratic gainer. On the one hand, inflation had been curbed and its *raison d'être* seems to have passed; on the other hand, the ESB was considered too powerful, with functions that overlapped with those of the regular ministries. These functions were for the most part decentralised into the Ministries of Economic Affairs and Communications and the Bank of Taiwan; this decentralisation followed a report on administrative reform designed to reduce redundancy and to revitalise the line ministries of the executive yuan. Since these ministries did not have the expertise or manpower to engage in planning, this reorganisation appeared to sacrifice an integrated approach to economic management.

In fact, the functions of macroeconomic planning and the utilisation of aid, as well as elements of the Industrial Development Commission, were shifted into the CUSA, which became the new super-ministry. Chaired by Chen Cheng, heir apparent at the time to Chiang Kai-shek, the CUSA orchestrated the third four-year plan and engineered most of the important reforms between 1958 and 1961 that are associated with the turn towards export-led growth [*Wang, 1993: 148*].

Planning was further recentralised in 1963 with the formation of the CIECD, which was responsible for the fourth and fifth five-year plans (1965–68 and 1969–72) as well as the drafting of the sixth one (1973–76). Vice-premier Wang Yung-wu and some legislators believed that the CUSA had over-extended itself, with too many subdivisions and small groups that needed consolidation. The end of US aid also demanded new activities, including soliciting foreign direct investment and coordinating foreign borrowing, and the development of the capacity to carry out planning exercises without the tutelage of the US aid mission.

Initially chaired by Chen Cheng, vice-president and premier, and then after his death by Yen in 1964, the CIECD appeared to be a new super-ministry. The CIECD was responsible for sectoral planning, borrowing from abroad, and endowed with its own resources in the form of the Sino-American Fund made of residual aid and counterpart funds. In fact, the CIECD was more like a coordinating body than a centralised agency like Korea's Economic Planning Board. During the period of the CIECD, economic technocrats and their extra-bureaucratic niches were gradually incorporated into the regular bureaucracy and the line ministries expanded their functions.[5]

The passing of the first generation of political leaders and the transfer of power to a new generation served to further weaken the CIECD. In 1969, vice premier Chiang Ching-kuo first became involved in economic issues by being assigned the chairmanship of the CIECD. The junior Chiang circumvented the CIECD by convening ad hoc meetings among line ministers to address major policy issues. In 1973, the CIECD was formally downgraded to vice-ministerial level and renamed the Economic Planning Council, while Chiang's informal meetings became institutionalised as a five-person Economic and Financial Special Group [*Wade, 1990: 200*]. Lacking in staff, the Special Group consisted of the Ministers of Finance and Economic Affairs, the governor of the Central Bank, the director-general of Budget, Accounting and Statistics, and the secretariat-general of the Executive Yuan. As in the 1958–63 period under the CUSA, planning was again decentralised to the line ministries, which regained power within their own bailiwicks, with loose coordination at the top [*Wen, 1984: 12–25*].

In 1978, when Y.S. Sun, then Minister of Economic Affairs, was appointed as premier, the EPC was again upgraded to ministerial rank and renamed the CEPD. One reason for the reorganisation was that Chiang Ching-kuo had by that time succeeded in placing his allies in the ministries. A second reason, however, was a growing concern about the need to steer the process of industrial upgrading and an interest on the part of some technocrats in emulating the Japanese and Korean models of more centralised industrial planning. Not coincidentally, the formation of the CEPD coincided with the rechartering of the Bank of Communication into a development bank and experimentation with sectorally targeted lending.

However, the contrasts between the CEPD and Korea's Economic Planning Board are even more instructive. The CEPD never regained the status of a superministry, such as the CUSA or CIECD; rather, it was on a par with the other ministries and provided coordinating functions. The CEPD did assess and approve large-scale development programmes and projects, such as the '10 major infrastructure projects' of the 1970s and the investments of the larger SOEs. But the agency was initially headed by the governor of the Central Bank, and his deputies tended to be economists; as a result, the CEPD was slow to embrace industrial policy as a primary objective. To the contrary, it became the locus for the push to internationalise and liberalise the economy, that gained strength as trade surpluses and foreign pressure mounted over the 1980s.

Under these organisational circumstances, it was the Industrial Development Bureau (IDB) of the Ministry of Economics Affairs that emerged as the leading advocate and practitioner of industrial policy. IDB organised export cartels, tried to have input in the screening of loans from the strategic industry fund, and maintained close dialogue with private-sector firms in targeted sectors. The IDB often found itself at loggerheads with the CEPD on issues such as trade policy. As the opportunities for protection or the manipulation of rules governing foreign direct investment narrowed, the IDB shifted its ground towards the promotion of collaborative R&D efforts in promising industries such as electronics, and as the organiser of capacity reduction in sectors experiencing economic distress. Beginning in the 1980s, it designated information and machinery as two strategic sectors for promotion.

There are several features of this organisational history that are noteworthy. First, the apparent complexity of the organisational structure and the constant changes they appeared to undergo was offset by a system that resembled interlocking directorates. For example, in 1955 the members of the Economic Stabilisation Board included the Governor of Taiwan (chair), the ministers of Finance, Economic Affairs, Communications and National Defense, the chairman of the Joint Committee on Rural Reconstruction, the secretary-general of the CUSA, the commissioner of Finance of Taiwan provincial government, the chairman of the board of the Bank of Taiwan, and the chairman of the Industrial Development Commission. A similar story can be told for the CUSA. Such overlaps created greater cohesion in the economic bureaucracy than might be at first apparent.

A second feature of this economic policy structure was its unusual organisational independence. With their budgets supported by US aid, the institutions analysed here enjoyed a degree of financial independence. Not only were the agencies financially independent; they were also exempted from normal civil service regulations, and were thus able to pay much higher salaries in the early 1950s, as much as five times as high. This enabled the agencies to recruit and train highly competent staff, to attract talent, and to maintain an organisational *esprit de corps*.

This organisational autonomy had operational consequences that are summarised by Neil Jacoby [*1966: 61*] in a discussion of the CUSA:

> Being free of the need to obtain legislative approval of its expenditures, the Council was able to act speedily on developmental projects ... Whereas the top councils of the Chinese government were preoccupied with political and military problems of security and 'return to the mainland', the Council could concentrate upon the development of Taiwan ... Had US aid been part of the Chinese government's budget, and administered through the regular departments of government, its developmental effects would have been greatly diminished.

A third feature of this structure was its surprising openness to penetration by American aid officials, who further served to coordinate policy informally. American officials sat in on the meetings of the Economic Stabilisation Board, Committee on United States Aid, Joint Committee on Rural Reconstruction, and the Foreign Exchange and Trade Commission. Chinese officials actually had to hold meetings in English for the benefit of American advisors, who would formally and informally make their case for particular reforms [*Gold, 1986: 68–9*]. The result was a particularly strong transnational alliance among aid donors and portions of the host government.

Personnel Policies

Until the 1980s, all ministers of finance and economic affairs and the heads of the economic planning agencies as well as most of their high-ranking subordinates were mainlanders who had come to Taiwan with the defeated KMT government. An interesting feature of this first generation of technocrats was the predominance of scientists and engineers. Economic technocrats trained in the social sciences – and known as 'economists' – occupied either lesser positions in industrial and fiscal policy areas or high positions only in finance and the banking sector. Of ten key decision-makers in Taiwan's post-war economic development, seven were scientists or engineers; of 19 other policy makers, 12 were [*Pang, 1992: Appendix A*].

Thanks to a recent study by Liu [*1989: 89–91*], we have a statistical comparison between 44 economic policy-makers and bureaucrats in the major economic policy-making institutions in the 1950s and 1960s with the 1957 members of the Central Standing Committee (CSC) of the KMT. Ninety-eight per cent of the planners had a university education, while the proportion for the party members was a surprisingly high 70 per cent. Fifty-two per cent of the planners had studied in the United States, as compared with 28 per cent of the CSC members. These data suggest that the top planning staff, though often educated in engineering and science rather than economics, had a more cosmopolitan and liberal outlook than their political counterparts [*Yang, 1984: 161–3*].

Many of the first generation of economic technocrats joined the government through the National Resource Commission, an agency created by the KMT regime on the mainland to oversee SOEs. On Taiwan, the economic technocrats in charge of industrial development came to favour private enterprise at a time when many officials in the government remained committed to a large SOE sector. Nonetheless, their outlook was hardly *laisser-faire*; rather, they looked to Meiji Japan as a role model [*Wang, 1993: 86-7,91*] and focused on the development and implementation of particular projects rather than on broad allocative efficiency [*Chu, 1986:*

30–33]. Into the 1980s, this engineering approach to industrial policy predominated [*Wade, 1990: 225–6*].

The *economists* in the government – and advising it – were divided into two groups: one with a monetarist-cum-neoclassical perspective called 'the academics' because most of their leading members have been based in universities abroad or the Academia Sinica; the other a Keynesian one dubbed the 'editorial group' because of their use of newspaper commentary as a vehicle for policy advocacy [*Commercial Times, 1982*]. The leading economic technocrats naturally found the editorial group more congenial than the academics, and they were instrumental in drafting the first few economic plans. But their influence weakened after the 1958–61 economic reforms, and over time they became increasingly critical of the government for lacking the kind of industrial and trade policies found in Korea [*Wang, 1988*].

From the very beginning of the country's post-war history, a number of the 'academics' held influential advisory positions, particularly with respect to macroeconomic policy-making [*Cheng, 1993: 86; Haggard and Pang, 1994*]. Academics were responsible for crucial elements of the stabilisation programme of the early 1950s, including the decision to pursue a high interest rate policy, the 1958 foreign exchange regime reform, the tax reform of 1968–69, and the liberalisation of financial markets that began in the mid-1970s. The academics were also consistent critics of government intervention in support of industry [*Hsing, 1993*] and, although these criticisms did not prevail, they constituted a check on 'high-powered' industrial policy that was largely absent within the government in Korea until the 1980s.

The expansion of the economic bureaucracy in the 1950s generated demand for new staff.[6] Recruits came predominantly from elite universities, particularly the National Taiwan University, and were trained in regular disciplines – engineering (for the industrial development bureau), economics and law – rather than through special professional programmes for the civil service, as is the case in Japan and France. Because of the bureaucratic independence of the early economic agencies, most new recruits were able to bypass the civil service examination, which continued to test knowledge of political ideology and classical Chinese. As the economic agencies were increasingly incorporated back into the formal bureaucratic structure, more new recruits passed through the civil service examination process, although direct hires from top-ranking universities continued until 1986, when the CEPD was formally 'bureaucratised'.

Passing the civil service examination in Taiwan does not confer the same degree of prestige as it does in Korea. Bureaucratic careers were initially limited to mainlanders, and later carried the implication of collaboration with the mainlander-dominated government. Aspiring Taiwanese thus sought alternative career paths, including the pursuit of advanced study and careers abroad. Partly as a result, the civil service examination was not as competitive as several other professional examinations (as measured by the failure rate), including the bar, the medical profession and accounting. Moreover, the civil service examination process remained tarnished by political exceptionalism, including 'back door' examinations to funnel KMT party elites and retired military officers into state bureaucracies and special provincial quotas for descendants of mainlanders.[7]

However, entry into the economic bureaucracies has been more selective than that for the general administration. Direct hiring from elite universities, particularly National Taiwan University, already implied that candidates had been through a rigorous screening process, namely the united entrance examination for college admission and, typically, also the masters programme in economics [*Cheng, 1992*]. Direct recruitment allowed the CEPD and other agencies to pick their recruits, while new entrants into the general civil service were assigned by the personnel department of the Examination Yuan. Moreover, there was no 'backdoor' entry into the economic agencies for party cadres or retired military personnel, nor any special quotas for mainlanders.

Compensation schemes have increasingly been seen as a crucial component of attracting talent and building a competent civil service. Until recently, however, pay in the public sector was from 30 to 50 per cent lower than that in the private sector [*Wade, 1990: 219, 280*]. Aversion to inflation and the very size of the public sector – as high as 17.5 per cent of the non-agricultural work force, not counting the military – limited the government's willingness to match private-sector salaries. Only after the mid-1980s did pay differentials between the public and private sectors begin to narrow.

Throughout the post-war period, however, technocrats in the economic planning agencies – most of which were associated with the US Aid Mission in one way or another – have been better paid than their counterparts in line ministries, such as the Ministry of Economic Affairs (MOEF) and Ministry of Finance (MOF). In the beginning of the 1950s, pay for employees on the Economic Stabilisation Board and in the Council on US Aid were five times higher than for those in regular bureaucracies [*Fu et al., 1967: 944*]. After the termination of US economic aid, the Sino-American Fund continued to cover the overhead of economic planning agencies. With the incorporation of economic bureaucracy into the government, the remunerative gap narrowed, but only gradually. In 1965 the salary of economic planners was twice that of their colleagues in line ministries [*Wang, 1993: 211*]. In the early 1970s, the gap still stood at 50 per cent. Only after 1986 were the CEPD pay scales standardised with those in the MOEF. However, as the pay gap narrowed, recruits in the economic bureaucracy were put on a fast track of promotion and became the core of the emerging leadership, now approaching the rank of vice-ministers.

II. KOREA

Under Syngman Rhee the bureaucracy was generally both ineffective and disorganised, characterised by widespread corruption and patronage. Not only were policy instruments used for political purposes, but the staffing of the bureaucracy itself was an important form of patronage [*Suh, 1967*]. The aggregate picture demands some modification, however, since portions of the bureaucracy were open to innovation and planning. The Korean bureaucracy in the late-1950s might be described as 'dualistic': technically-oriented 'developmental enclaves' existed, but their functioning was circumscribed by the political interference of the top leadership [*Lee, 1968*].

In 1955, Rhee established the Ministry of Reconstruction (MOR). As a counterpart to the US aid mission, the purpose of the MOR was to develop plans that could be used to nail down US aid commitments over a longer time horizon. The first Minister of Reconstruction was Son In-sang, an ex-banker with experience at the World Bank. The MOR was involved in the coordination of annual stabilisation plans with the American aid mission through the revived Combined Economic Board, which provided a working link with foreign advisors interested in rationalising economic management.

In general, however, institutions and politics in Korea made the Rhee government less amenable to reform than the KMT regime in Taiwan. In contrast to Taiwan, the United States had imposed a set of weak democratic institutions on Korea. Syngman Rhee was not above political manipulation and it is generous to consider the political system democratic in any but a formal sense [*Palais, 1973; Henderson, 1968*]. None the less, Rhee did have to play an electoral game. One obvious way of mobilising funds to finance elections and other party activities was to forge a closer alliance with the new businessmen who had risen in the post-World War II period through commerce or the acquisition of SOEs. The erratic nature of economic policy and the extensive corruption in the 1950s can be seen as an outcome of this effort to build bases of business support [*Haggard, Cooper and Moon, 1993*].

It was thus not until 1958 that domestic planning efforts got under way, influenced by the Indian model [*Lee, 1968; Wolf, 1962*]. An Economic Development Council (EDC) was formed in March 1958 as a consulting and research agency for the Ministry of Reconstruction, financed partly by counterpart funds. In April 1959, the EDC economists drafted a Three Year

Plan which was to be the foundation for later planning efforts. The macroeconomic framework was a relatively sophisticated one that stressed employment objectives and based investment requirements on specified capital-labour ratios by sector. The plan spurred reforms in the government's statistical capabilities and became an important educational device, even if its technical sophistication far outstripped the government's capacity to implement it.

The fate of the Three Year Plan was decided by politics both within and outside the bureaucracy. The semi-independent status of the EDC created interministerial jealousies, particularly with the Ministry of Finance, which resisted MOR efforts to extend its authority. Additional problems were raised by the relative youth and low rank of the reform group. The nature of the broader political milieu guaranteed that support for the reformers would not be forthcoming. The economic bureaucracy as a whole had little autonomy from pressures emanating from the ruling party, the private sector and the executive itself.

Conditions only worsened as the political situation deteriorated over the late 1950s. Preoccupied with political problems, Rhee reviewed the Three Year Plan only twice during the two-year period of its formulation. Besieged by political difficulties in 1959, the Liberal Party shelved the final draft of the plan for a year, approving it only a few days before the student revolution of 1960 that ended Liberal Party rule. The last years of the Rhee administration were thus a period of some innovation within the economic bureaucracy, but these innovations took place in a larger political context that blocked reform.

Military Centralisation

Upon seising power, the military undertook a substantial restructuring of the bureaucracy and the economic decision-making structure [*Cho, 1968; Kim, 1988; Haggard, Cooper and Moon, 1993*]. The change of government provided an auspicious opening for reformers within the bureaucracy to push forward the ideas concerning administrative restructuring that had already been developed under Rhee. The reformers' plans for an Economic Planning Board (EPB) fit with the centralising tendencies of the military, resulting in a ministry that had an unusual level of intra-bureaucratic independence and control over the activities of other ministries. The bureaucratic reform centralised control over a variety of policy instruments, including control over foreign exchange, finance, trade policy, and the budget.

The new ministry consisted of the budget bureau, transferred from the Ministry of Finance, the statistics and research bureau, moved from the Ministry of Home Affairs, and the planning coordination offices from the

MOR. From its initiation, however, the EPB came to have a powerful say over other ministries through the budget. The EPB's Bureau of Budget prepares the broad guidelines for the annual budget, collects annual proposals from the other ministries and evaluates their feasibility. The EPB's power lies in its ability to designate specific projects for which other ministries prepare the budgetary implications and, above all, in its power to adjust the budget estimates submitted by the ministries, which generally exceed that called for by the total budget. The EPB then passes the budget on to the president for approval, and though the National Assembly is given 60 days to deliberate on the budget, it has had little power to alter the budget's structure, even following the transition to democratic rule in the 1980s.

A capital import bureau was also established in 1961, and the EPB's power extended to the area of foreign borrowing. In July 1962, the ministry was given the power to grant government guarantees to loans and to audit and oversee the activities of the borrowing firms. When coupled with the power to approve and extend incentives to foreign direct investment and the ability to select those capital goods imports and importers which qualified for government-aided deferred payment privileges, the new ministry effectively gained complete control over capital inflows.

These laws effectively gave the EPB a strong say over the money supply as well. As Sylvia Maxfield shows in some detail, the Korean Finance Minister was effectively subordinated to the EPB and the Central Bank was subordinated to the Ministry of Finance [*Maxfield, forthcoming*]. But the EPB's influence over the financial system did not stop there; because the government owned the banking system, monetary and credit policies were ancillary to industrial policy objectives. Preferential finance became a central tool of government industrial policy [*Woo, 1990; Choi, 1993*], with its end use ultimately dictated by the planning apparatus headquartered in the EPB.

In 1963, the special status of the EPB within the cabinet was further enhanced when its minister was also given the title of deputy prime minister. At the same time, an Economic Ministers' Meeting and an Economic Vice-Ministers' Meeting were created, for which the EPB served as the support staff. Ministries established special ad hoc committees for the analysis of certain policy issues, and private experts could participate in such committees, but these committees generally approved policies proposed by the ministry.

In addition to consolidating the economic planning structure itself, the military government also forged much closer relations between the executive and the economic policy machinery more generally; there could be little question that the president was firmly in command [*Wolf, 1962*]. On coming to power, the military demanded weekly briefings on the state of the economy. The military had developed a standard briefing procedure, leading to the joke that the country was run by the 'ABCs': Army, briefings and charts. These briefings provided an important channel of access for the technocrats, however, and a way of influencing and educating the top military leaders. The close interest in economic developments was visible after 1964 in the construction of an 'economic situation room' that allowed Park to monitor progress on specific projects on a daily, and even hourly, basis, and in the organisation of four Presidential Secretariats within the Blue House, the presidential mansion. Two dealt with political, two with economic affairs. Recruited from the ministries, the secretaries and special assistants allowed Park to maintain close contact with, and control over, the bureaucracy. The contrast with Rhee's aloofness from the details of economic management is striking.

The military also developed a system of 'planning and control offices' (PCOs) as a way of monitoring and evaluating performance. A PCO was established within the EPB in July 1961 and the model was gradually extended to other ministries. Placed under an Office of Planning Coordination in the Prime Minister's office, the PCOs were required to monitor and evaluate the status of implementation of its projects in quarterly reports. These in turn were evaluated by an outside Economic Performance Evaluation Group. This system constituted an intricate web that linked ministries horizontally while giving the prime minister, and ultimately the president, another independent channel of information on the bureaucracy and specific projects.

The ends to which these bureaucratic reforms were to be put rested on a restructuring of business–government relations. After the fall of the Rhee government, the punishment of those who had illicitly accumulated wealth during the 1950s became a major political issue [*Kim, 1967*]. Two weeks after the coup, the junta arrested 13 major businessmen. Though eight of these were induced to make large 'contributions' to the government and were released, the investigation was broadened to include another 120 businessmen. The definition of 'illicit' wealth accumulation was inclusive, covering the entire range of rent-seeking and rent-granting activities that had been pervasive, if not unavoidable, under Rhee. Moreover, radical members of the junta were arguing that all illegally accumulated fortunes should be confiscated outright and the profiteers put before a firing squad.

The government did seize all outstanding shares of commercial bank stocks, thus gaining direct control of an important institution. Bargains were ultimately struck with large manufacturing and construction firms, however. The reason is summarised neatly by Kim [*1967: 470*]: '... the only viable economic force happened to be the target group of leading entrepreneurial talents with their singular advantage of organisation, personnel, facilities and capital resource'. On their release, the members of the newly formed Korean Businessmen's Association submitted a plan to the Supreme Council identifying 14 key industrial plants – cement, steel, fertiliser, cable, etc. – in which they were interested in investing if the appropriate supportive policies were forthcoming. In making peace with the newly organised private sector, the new bureaucratic organisation was put into the service of the outward-oriented but interventionist policy style that has been thoroughly documented in the literature on Korea.

Despite the centralisation of economic functions, the EPB and the other economic ministries did not constitute the totality of the economic bureaucracy. Park continued to rely on, and seek support from, the military. No military personnel held the Ministry of Finance under Park Chung Hee, but 11 out of 16 transportation ministers, nine out of 13 ministers of home affairs and six out of 15 construction ministers were military men. In effect, Park Chung-hee created a bifurcated bureaucracy, in which domestic 'service' ministries, such as construction, were staffed with clientelistic appointments, allowed to be relatively inefficient, and served to satisfy domestic patronage requirements [*Kang, 1997*].

Personnel Policy and the Organisation of the Civil Service

Organisational reform was matched by an overhaul of the civil service. The Americans had sought civil service reform under the Rhee regime, but as a detailed study [*Bark, 1967: 221–2*] concludes, it 'was difficult to find any effect of the American effort on the personnel system in Korea'. The military government undertook reforms both by purging the bureaucracy and by reforming recruitment procedures.

Under the military junta, the 'Extraordinary Measures for National Reconstruction Law' allowed the suspension of all civil rights. Under this law, 2,000 military officers, including 55 generals, were dismissed on charges of factionalism and corruption [*Henderson, 1968: 183*] and the Political Purification Law of 1962 barred 4,369 persons from political activity. The junta also dismissed 35,684 civil servants on various charges [*Lee, 1968: 310*]. Even a decade later, when Park's rule was relatively consolidated, Park dismissed 331 officials in April 1974 for corruption, including 52 with posts higher than section chief. In March 1977, 420 civil servants were purged. In 1976, 15,000 officials were reprimanded and sanctioned for corruption. The willingness of the president to directly intervene was visible under President Chun Doo-hwan (1980–86) as well. Even before Chun took power, he headed a 'Special Commission for National Security Measures' that purged 4,760 public officials in late 1979 [*Kang, 1997*].

Under the guidance of the Minister of Cabinet Administration, a series of reforms under the military rationalised the system of personnel administration and moved towards a more meritocratic system. As a study conducted by the US aid mission noted, 'with the advent of the military government the door to personnel administration improvements swung open' [*Landers, 1967: 85*]. These included: centralising recruitment and selection; improving examinations; installing a performance rating system; adapting a new training system; improving pay administration and installing a position classification system.

Passing the higher civil service exam in Korea has historically carried tremendous prestige, and competition under both Rhee and Park was fierce. The ratio of successful applicants to those taking the exam were daunting: in 1949 there were 100 exam-takers for every successful applicant; in 1956, 214; in 1957, 315. Under Rhee, however, higher civil servants frequently bypassed the examination process altogether and were increasingly recruited with only perfunctory screening; patronage and political appointments prevailed. From 1949 to 1961, only 336 men passed qualifying tests, compared to 8,263 'special appointments' [*Park, 1961; Song, 1960; Yi, 1966; Kang, 1997*]. While only 4.1 per cent of higher civil servants under Rhee entered the bureaucracy through merit-based examinations, a full 20 per cent entered that way under Park and the number of internal promotions, governed to a greater extent by merit, also increased at the top ranks [*Cho, 1968*].

As in Taiwan, civil servants in Korea generally earn less than their counterparts in the private sector. A 1992 World Bank report found that pay, even at the senior level, was roughly 70 per cent that of a private sector official. In contrast to Taiwan, however, Korea does not appear to have had extra-bureaucratic career routes that permitted extraordinary compensation for top civil servants except for a small group of officials in the late 1950s who were working in aid-related ministries. However, pay discrepancies do not include illegal or quasi-legal compensation to which middle- and top-level bureaucrats have had access. Until the implementation of a 'clean government' campaign by President Kim Young-sam in the 1990s, it was generally accepted for business to provide gifts, services and even cash for bureaucrats as a way of keeping relations with various ministries on a solid footing. In contrast to Taiwan, there is also a moderate amount of Japanese-style *amakudari* (descent from heaven) in Korea, a system through which retired bureaucrats assume positions in the private sector upon retirement and thus effectively increase their lifetime earnings. Government officials have also often found positions in various quasi-governmental organisations.

The Heavy Industry Drive

Even though Park supported and protected the economic technocrats, it is a mistake to see them as independent from the executive. The decision to launch the Heavy and Chemical Industry Plan (hereafter called the 'Plan') in the early 1970s provides an example of how the political objectives of the executive could prevail over, and ultimately circumvent, the economic bureaucracy.

Military calculations undoubtedly weighed heavily in Park's calculations to launch the heavy industry push [*Rhee, 1991*]. Nixon's 'Guam Doctrine' of 1969 appeared to signal American retreat from East Asia, and was followed closely by the withdrawal of one infantry division from Korea in March 1971. Heavy industries, such as steel and machinery, would form the core of a defence-industrial complex capable of guaranteeing Korea's defence self-reliance.

However, the Plan also appeared to have a domestic political rationale. In 1972, in response to growing protest against the autocratic style of his rule, Park restructured politics in an explicitly authoritarian direction with the imposition of the Yushin, or 'revitalising', Constitution. This political change was followed by two major economic policy initiatives designed to secure new bases of political support: an expansion of the Saemaul (New Village) Movement that improved rural welfare and cemented Park's standing among his conservative rural constituents; and the ambitious Plan that benefited the largest Korean firms, or *chaebol*. Both the Saemual movement and the formulation and implementation of the Plan bypassed existing bureaucratic structures by creating new ones directly responsible to the president [*Choi, 1987*].

The decision-making structure surrounding the Plan established the key intra-bureaucratic cleavages of the late 1970s, contributed to the incoherence of macroeconomic policy, and was an important factor behind the increasing intervention of the state in the economy [*Choi, 1987; Rhee, 1991*]. During the first half of 1973, the Plan was drafted by a small working group centred in the Blue House. Working closely with the industry-oriented Ministry of Commerce and Industry, the formulation of the Plan bypassed both the EPB and the MOF. It was released in May, at which time a Heavy and Chemical Industry Promotion Committee was formed under the Office of the Prime Minister. This organisational arrangement was unusual. The committee included all major economic ministers, but departed from the usual practice of centring economic policy coordination around the EPB.

In September, a Heavy and Chemical Industry Planning Council was formed which later came under the direction of the Second Presidential

Economic Secretary Oh Won Chul, an engineer with a decade of experience in the industrial bureaucracy. Oh Won Chul was a strong advocate of an extremely activist industrial policy that would involve the government in detailed sectoral planning. The Planning Council was an extremely powerful body. Designed to provide staff work to the Committee, it was also the centre of various interministerial working groups designed to assist implementation of the plan and the main point of contact for consultations with big business over specific projects.

Numerous instruments were deployed in support of the plan, but the central policy instrument was preferential credit. Though managed by the banks, the allocation of funds was largely in the hands of the Planning Council and ultimately with the president himself, who exercised final approval over major projects. The Plan, and the system for managing it, thus had important implications for the conduct of macroeconomic policy, since crucial decisions affecting the level and allocation of credit took place outside of the normal planning channels in which the EPB and the Ministry of Finance played a more central role. In 1974 the Ministry of Finance created a massive National Investment Fund through mandatory deposits from financial institutions. The immediate aim of the Fund was to finance the heavy industry plan, but for the Ministry of Finance it also served the political function of setting some limits on the ambition of industrial planners in a bureaucratic context in which direct opposition to the initiative was impossible. Not until a coincidence of economic and political difficulties of 1979 did the EPB regain its position within the bureaucratic hierarchy, as Park was finally forced to scale down his ambitious heavy industry drive [*Haggard et al., 1994*].

III. CONCLUSION

One must be cautious in drawing policy conclusions for other countries. To some extent, institutional structures constitute organic wholes: it is difficult to transplant one part without importing the entire system. Nonetheless, there are lessons to be drawn from these cases, lessons which underscore the importance of strengthening institutions as a component of the economic reform process.

First, although reform was typically preceded by a concentration of political power in the executive, executives also delegated some independent decision-making authority to relatively insulated technocratic agencies. Why did they choose to do this? Crisis conditions are an important part of the story. Typically, erratic policy and performance in previous periods had damaged the credibility of the government in the eyes of investors, bilateral donors and the multilateral financial institutions.

Delegation signalled the government's willingness to make certain policy decisions on the basis of economic criteria.

The importance of concentrated executive authority does not imply the necessity of authoritarian rule for successful reform; we now have important cases of democratic governments undertaking radical reforms, including Poland, Argentina and Bolivia. Yet it is interesting to note that these democratic reform episodes resemble in important ways the pattern of reform in Korea and Taiwan. Crises permitted a concentration of executive authority, albeit in a democratic context, which was coupled with a degree of delegation to technocratic agencies.

When we turn to the actual organisation of the economic bureaucracy, there is no single pattern. Korea's high degree of centralisation reflected the military's more interventionist policy style, and allowed the government to coordinate a range of policy instruments around the objective of rapid industrial growth. With this style came certain risks: macroeconomic policy was sometimes sacrificed to industrial policy objectives and as business concentration increased, policy-making shifted from the economic bureaucracy to the office of the president, and technocratic checks on policy diminished. The looser organisational pattern in Taiwan was mirrored in a less dirigist policy style, though we have shown that there was a variety of effective coordinating mechanisms: the US aid machinery, a strong central bank, 'interlocking directorates' and the creation of ad hoc coordinating bodies.

None the less, in both systems, political leaderships saw merit in insulating some portions of the economic bureaucracy from other branches of government and from interest group pressures. An important component of this insulation centred on personnel policy and an expansion of the meritocratic portion of the bureaucracy. Both countries also shared a pattern of civil service organisation that recruits from top educational institutions, promotes from within, and limits lateral entry, thus encouraging strong loyalty to organisational goals [*Evans, 1995*]. The two countries undertook somewhat different strategies in achieving this goal; the military in Korea attempted an overall reform of the civil service, while Taiwan relied to a greater extent on special career tracks that fell outside of the normal civil service. However, the common attention to building state capacity through strengthening of the civil service is a clear reminder that policy and institutional reform go hand in hand.

NOTES

1. At that time, the employees of the Council on Economic Planning and Development were finally integrated into the civil service and were no longer supported by the Sino-American Fund, a 'second budget' that had been established following the termination of US aid in 1964, that had operated beyond the scrutiny of the legislative branch.
2. A fourth important area concerned the organisations for agricultural development, the most interesting of which was the Joint [i.e. Chinese-American] Commission on Rural Reconstruction, which had virtual plenary powers in the agriculture reform area.
3. The Taiwan Production Board was nominally chaired by the governor of Taiwan, but was actually directed by the vice-chairman of the Board, K.Y. Yin, who was concurrently head of the Central Trust Bureau, a government financial institution [*Wang, 1995: 36*]. At its creation, the ESB also absorbed a central-government coordinating committee, the Committee on Economic and Financial Affairs (CEFA), and the commission of industrial development of the Council on United States Aid (described in more detail below). The CEFA was established in March 1951 to review and coordinate trade, payments, monetary and fiscal policies in the interest of stabilisation, and reflected the interest of the national government in asserting its authority over economic policy making.
4. The first was responsible for industrial development planning; the second was in charge of utilising US aid; the third assumed responsibility for controlling fiscal policy, including state-owned enterprises; the fourth undertook planning for agriculture, forestry and fishing; and the fifth was responsible for establishing policies for controlling price levels.
5. The Investment Group was reorganised as a Bureau of Investment Affairs, and its rank and file became civil servants [*Wang, 1993: 148*], while more and more full-time members of the CUSA and CIECD began to assume ministerial positions. An Industrial Development Bureau was created within the Ministry of Economic Affairs in 1968 and its Bureau of Commerce was expanded.
6. The following draws on an interview with Wang-an Yeh on 30 November 1995.
7. Interview with Tso-jung Wang on 1 December 1995.

REFERENCES

Amsden, A., 1989, *Asia's Next Giant*, New York: Oxford University Press.
Bark, D.S., 1967, 'Public Personnel Administration', unpublished Ph.D. dissertation, University of Minnesota, Duluth.
Campos, J.E. and H.L. Root, 1996, *The Key to the Asian Miracle: Making Shared Growth Credible*, Washington, DC: The Brookings Institution.
Chang, H.J., 1993, *The Political Economy of Industrial Policy*, New York: St. Martin's Press.
Cheng, T.J., 1990, 'Political Regimes and Development Strategies: South Korea and Taiwan', in G. Gereffi and D. Wyman (eds.), *Manufacturing Miracles: Patterns of Development in Latin American and East Asia*, Princeton, NJ: Princeton University Press.
Cheng, T.J., 1992, 'Dilemmas and Choices in Educational Policy: The Case of South Korea and Taiwan', *Studies in Comparative International Development*, Vol.27, No.4.
Cheng, T.J., 1993, 'Guarding the Commanding Heights: the State as Banker in Taiwan', in Stephan Haggard, Chung Lee and Sylvia Maxfield (eds.), *The Politics of Finance in Developing Countries*, Ithaca, NY: Cornell University Press.
Cho, S.C., 1968, 'Hankguk Kunsa Chongbu ha e issoso ui tugaji haengjong kaehyok e kwanhan pigyo yongu' (A Comparative Study of two administrative Reforms under the Korean Military Government), *Hanguk haengjong nonchong* (Korean Journal of Public Administration), Vol.6, No.2, June, pp.214–35.
Choi, B.S., 1987, 'Institutionalising a Liberal Economic Order in Korea: The Strategic Management of Economic Change', unpublished Ph.D. dissertation, Harvard University, Cambridge, MA.

Choi, B.S., 1993, 'Financial Policy and Big Business in Korea: The Perils of Financial Regulation', in Stephan Haggard, Chung Lee and Sylvia Maxfield (eds.), *The Politics of Finance in Developing Countries*, Ithaca, NY: Cornell University Press.

Commercial Times, 1982, *Ching-chi cheng-tse ta-pien-lun* (Grand Debates on Economic Policy), Taipei: China Times.

Evans, P., 1992, 'The state as problem and solution: Predation, embedded autonomy, and structural change', in Stephan Haggard and Robert Kaufman (eds.), *The Politics of Economic Adjustment: International Constraints, Distributive Conflicts, and the State*, Princeton, NJ: Princeton University Press.

Evans, P., 1995, *Embedded Autonomy: The State and Industrial Transformation*, Princeton, NJ: Princeton University Press.

Fu, Chi-hsueh *et al.*, 1967, *Chung-hua-min-kuo jian-cha-yuan chi yen-chiu* (The Control Yuan in the Republic of China), Taipei: no publisher.

Galenson, W. (ed.), 1979, *Economic Growth and Structural Change in Taiwan*, Ithaca, NY: Cornell University Press.

Geddes, B., 1994, *The Politicians' Dilemma: Reforming the State in Latin America*, Berkeley, CA: University of California Press.

Gereffi, G. and D.L. Wyman, 1990, *Manufacturing Miracles*, Princeton, NJ: Princeton University Press.

Gold, T., 1980, 'Dependent Development in Taiwan', unpublished Ph.D dissertation, Harvard University, Cambridge, MA.

Gold, T., 1986, *State and Society in the Taiwan Miracle*, Armonk, NY: M.E. Sharpe.

Haggard, Stephan, 1990, *Pathways from the Periphery: The Politics of Growth in the Newly Industrialising Countries*, Ithaca, NY: Cornell University Press.

Haggard, S. and C.K. Pang, 1994, 'The Transition to Export-Led Growth in Taiwan', in Joel D. Aberbach, David Dollar and Kenneth L. Sokoloff (eds.), *The Role of the State in Taiwan's Development*, Armonk, NY: M.E. Sharpe.

Haggard, S., Cooper, R. and C.I. Moon, 1993, 'Policy Reform in Korea', in Robert Bates and Anne Krueger (eds.), *Political and Economic Interactions in Economic Policy Reform*, Cambridge, MA: Blackwell Publishers.

Haggard, S. *et al.*, 1994, *Macroeconomic Policy and Performance in Korea, 1970–1990*, Cambridge, MA: Harvard University Press.

Henderson, G., 1968, *Korean Politics of the Vortex*, Cambridge, MA: Harvard University Press.

Hsing, M.H., 1993, *Taiwan ching-chi tse-lung* (On Taiwan's Economic Policies), Taipei: Sun-ming.

Jacoby, N., 1966, *US Aid to Taiwan: A Study of Foreign Aid, Self-Help, and Development*, New York: Praeger.

Johnson, C., 1982, *MITI and the Japanese Miracle: The Growth of Industrial Policy 1930-1970*, Stanford, CA: Stanford University Press.

Kang, D.C., 1997, 'Patronage Games: Politics and Bureaucracies in Korea and the Philippines' (unpublished), Hanover, New Hampshire (USA): Dartmouth College.

Kim, B.K., 1988, 'Bringing and Managing Socioeconomic Change: The State in Korea and Mexico', unpublished Ph.D. dissertation, Harvard University, Cambridge, MA.

Kim, Kyong-Dong, 1967, 'Political Factors in the Formation of the Entrepreneurial Elite in South Korea', *Asian Survey*, May.

Krueger, A.O., 1979, *The Developmental Role of the Foreign Sector and Aid*, Cambridge, MA: Harvard University Press.

Kuo, C.T., 1995, *Global Competitiveness and Industrial Growth in Taiwan and the Philippines*, Pittsburgh, PA: University of Pittsburgh Press.

Landers, F.M., 1967, *Technical Assistance in Public Administration: USOM/Korea, 1955–1967*, Seoul: USOM/Korea.

Lee, H.B., 1968, *Time, Change, Administration*, Honolulu, HI: East–West Center.

Liu, A.P.L., 1989, *Phoenix and the Lame Lion: Modernisation inn Taiwan and Mainland China 1950-80*, Stanford, CA: Hoover Institute Press.

Maxfield, S., forthcoming, *Letting Capital Loose*, Princeton, NJ: Princeton University Press.

Palais, J., 1973, 'Democracy in South Korea, 1948–1972', in Frank Baldwin (ed.), *Without*

Parallel: The American-South Korean Relationship since 1945, New York: Pantheon.

Pang, Chien-Kuo, 1992, *The State and Economic Transformation: The Taiwan Case*, New York: Garland.

Rhee, Jong-chan, 1991, 'The Limits of Authoritarian State Capacities: The State-Controlled Capitalist Collective Action for Industrial Adjustment in Korea, 1973–1987', Ph.D. dissertation, University of Pennsylvania, Philadelphia.

Song, W.Y., 1960, 'Kyongmudaeui inui changmak' (Behind the Veil of the Blue House), *Sasang'gye*, June.

Suh, B.D., 1967, 'Public Personnel Administration in Korea', unpublished Ph.D thesis, Duluth, USA: University of Minnesota.

Wade, R.L., 1990, *Governing the Market*, Princeton, NJ: Princeton University Press.

Wang, L.S., 1993, *Li Kuo-ting kou-shu li-shih: hua-so tai-wan ching-yen* (The K.T. Li Oral History of Taiwan's Economic Development), Taipei: Jou-yueh.

Wang, T.J., 1988, *Chai-ching wen-chun sang-pen* (Selected Essays on Taiwan's Finance and Economy), Taipei: China Times.

Wang, V.W.C., 1995, 'High Technology and Development Strategies in East Asia and Latin America', unpublished Ph.D. dissertation, University of Chicago.

Wen, H.S., 1984, 'Ching-chien-hui ti kuo-chu, hsien-tsai, yu wei-lai', *Tien-hsia*, Vol.42, pp.12–25.

Wolf, C. Jr., 1962, 'Economic Planning in Korea', *Asian Survey*, Dec.

Woo, J.E., 1990, *Race to the Swift*, New York: Columbia University Press.

Yang, H.S., 1984, 'Taiwan ching-chi ti lin-hang-jen' (The Pilots of Taiwan's Economy), in *T'ou-shih ching chi ch'iang-jen* (Gaining a Perspective of the Economic Strong Men), Taipei: Ching-chi-jen tsa-chi she.

Yen, Yen-chun, 1989, *Tsau-nien chi tai-wan* (Taiwan in its Early Post-War Years), Taipei: China Times.

Yi, M.Y., 1996, 'Kongmuwon pup'ae isipnyonsa' (Twenty Years of Civil Service Corruption), *Sasang'gye*, March.

Savings, Investment and the Corporation in the East Asian Miracle

AJIT SINGH

Most economists will accept that high rates of accumulation have been a key factor in East Asian economic success. This contribution explores specifically the reasons for extremely high rates of corporate savings and investments achieved by these economies. It focuses on the private corporation, the relationship between the corporation and the government and that between the corporation and the financial system. It analyses the nature of the investments–profits–savings nexus in Japan and Korea and indicates its contribution towards resolving the main macro-economic constraints on economic growth.

INTRODUCTION

Although there is considerable controversy concerning the reasons for fast economic growth in East Asia, most economists accept that high rates of savings and investments in these countries have been a key factor in their economic success.[1] East Asian countries top the international league tables not just with respect to the long-term growth of their GDP but also in relation to their national savings and investment rates. The latter was however not always the case. In the 1950s and 1960s many of these countries had much lower savings and investment rates than developing countries elsewhere, for example in Latin America. The South Korean annual domestic savings rate between 1955 and 1965 averaged only 3.3 per cent of GDP compared, for instance, with 14.8 per cent in Mexico, 16 per cent in Brazil and 21 per cent in Peru. However, between 1990 and 1994 South Korea recorded an average domestic savings rate of more than 35 per cent of GDP. The corresponding savings rates in the early 1990s for Mexico, Brazil and Peru were 17.2 per cent, 20.4 per cent and 18.9 per cent respectively.

Ajit Singh, Faculty of Economics, University of Cambridge, Cambridge, England.

Further, it is also significant that not only do East Asian countries have very impressive overall savings and investment rates but, relative to other countries, they have been particularly successful in achieving very high corporate savings and investments. The more or less comparable flow-of-funds data, which are unfortunately only available for a small group of developing countries, suggest for example that in the early 1980s business investment was 22 per cent of GNP in China, 20 per cent in Korea, 16 per cent in Malaysia, 15 per cent in Thailand, compared with 10 per cent in Columbia and 11 per cent in Ecuador. Similarly, business savings as a proportion of GNP in the East Asian countries were considerably greater than in the Latin American economies [*Honohan and Atiyas, 1993*].

This contribution explores the reasons for these high corporate savings and investment rates in East Asia. It does so by considering in some detail specifically the case of Japan between 1950 and 1973, and of Korea. It provides *inter alia* an analytical and empirical commentary on the thesis of Akyüz *et al.* [*1997*], which stresses the role of profits in the dynamics of the accumulation process in East Asian countries. The private corporation itself – unfortunately a much neglected subject in development economics [*Singh, 1995d*] – and specifically the relationship between the corporation and the government and that between the corporation and the financial system are the central focus of this study. It provides an analysis of how corporate savings, profits and investments in the reference countries contributed to their overall national objectives of obtaining an equality of *ex ante* savings and investment as well as of a current account equilibrium at high rates of long-term economic growth.

I. INVESTMENTS–PROFITS–SAVINGS NEXUS IN JAPAN DURING 1950–73

We consider first at the broad aggregate level the relationship between investment, profits and savings in Japan during 1950 to 1973, a period chosen because of its relevance for developing countries. In the early 1950s, the Japanese level of industrialisation was not all that different from that of many semi-industrial countries today. As a consequence of the extraordinary economic growth in the 1950s and 1960s – when Japanese industrial production expanded at a phenomenal rate of about 13 per cent per annum, GDP at ten per cent per annum and its share in world exports of manufacture rose by a huge ten percentage points – by the early 1970s, Japan had graduated to the status of being an advanced industrial country. The Japanese experience since 1973, although it still has implications for developing countries, is not as directly significant as the earlier period.

Table 1 shows the extremely high aggregate investment rates attained in

TABLE 1
GROSS FIXED INVESTMENT RATIOS, 1953–72
(Percentage of GNP at constant prices)

	Total fixed capital formation	Excluding residential construction	Trend increase in total share[a]
Japan	31.8	26.2	1.11
France	23.0	17.1	0.66
Germany	25.1	19.4	0.25
Italy	20.2	14.2	(0.03)
United Kingdom	17.3	14.1	0.40
United States	17.0	12.8	(−0.02)
Soviet Union	17.0	12.8	0.28[b]

Source: Boltho [*1975*].

Notes: a Annual increase in share of total gross fixed investment in GNP obtained by fitting linear time trends to the data. Figures in brackets are statistically not significant at the 5 per cent confidence level.
b Total fixed investment as a share of NMP (1950–69).

TABLE 2
GROSS SAVINGS RATIOS, 1953–72
(Percentage of GNP at current prices)

	Total	Household[a]	Corporations[b]	Government
Japan	36.9	15.8	13.5	7.8[b]
France	25.0	10.2	10.4	4.3
Germany	27.1	9.6	11.2[c]	6.3
Italy[d]	23.4	12.6	9.7[c]	1.1
United Kingdom	18.3	5.0	8.8	4.3
United States	18.0	8.0	7.7	2.4[b]
Finland	28.4	10.0	9.6	8.9
Netherlands	27.1	9.1	12.9[c]	5.1
Switzerland[e]	28.3	12.6	10.2	5.4

Source: Boltho [*1975*].

Notes: a   Including unincorporated enterprises.
b   Including public corporations.
c   Including depreciation allowances of unincorporated enterprises.
e   1961–72.
e   1953–69.

Japan during the 1950s and 1960s, compared with other leading industrial economies.[2] Even excluding residential construction, Japan invested on average more than a quarter of its GDP between 1953 and 1972. Further disaggregation of these data indicate that Japan invested eight per cent of GDP in the manufacturing sector in this period as against four per cent in Britain and six to seven per cent (including investment in the construction sector) in France and Germany [*Boltho, 1975*]. Table 2, on gross aggregate and sectoral savings ratios, shows that the average savings propensities of each of the three (household, business and government) sectors in Japan was higher, often by a considerable margin, than those in most other countries.

What accounts for these high Japanese savings and investment rates, particularly in the corporate sector? It will be argued here that essentially there were two major forces at work:

(1) The relationship between government and business which played a critical role in different ways in ensuring that corporate profits, as well as propensities to save and invest, increased over time and remained at a high level.

(2) The nature of the Japanese corporate organisation and the relationship between the corporation and the financial system. These were important in ensuring that the Japanese corporations were able to take a long-term view in their investment decisions.

Policies adopted under both (1) and (2) will be examined below.

(1) State Intervention and Profits

Table 3 indicates that at the macroeconomic level Japan had a much higher share of profits in the total output as well as considerably higher profit rates than other industrial countries in the reference period. In 1970 gross profits constituted more than a half of gross manufacturing value added in Japan compared with less than a quarter in the United Kingdom and United States, and about a third in countries like Germany and Italy. National accounts statistics suggest that the story is much the same if the comparison is made on the basis of net rather than gross profits. Moreover, there is evidence that during 1955–73 most sample countries had a trend decline in profit share, while Japan recorded a small trend increase (although it was not statistically significant) [*Hill, 1979*].

TABLE 3
GROSS PROFITS AND RATES OF RETURNS:
MANUFACTURING INDUSTRIAL COUNTRIES, 1955–72

		1955	1960	1965	1970	1972
Canada	P/Y	35.6	33.4	34.4	30.2	32.3
	P/K	19.3	15.3	15.4	12.5	13.8
United States	P/Y	28.0	27.0	29.5	23.5	26.1
	P/K	24.1	21.7	27.1	18.0	20.4
Japan	P/Y	43.9	51.8	47.6	50.4	45.6
	P/K	19.9	32.8	26.0	30.9	25.1
Germany	P/Y	41.1	38.4	35.8	32.5	28.6
	P/K	24.0	21.9	19.0	17.1	13.9
Italy	P/Y	41.3	40.8	33.5	31.6	29.3
	P/K	12.8	12.0	9.1	10.2	9.0
Sweden	P/Y	31.3	32.5	29.9	33.0	28.0
	P/K	12.7	12.9	11.6	13.2	9.9
United Kingdom	P/Y	33.7	32.9	30.1	24.6	25.8
	P/K	13.6	13.7	11.8	8.8	8.6
Australia	P/Y	25.9	29.1	34.4	33.4	29.5
Denmark	P/Y	42.1	47.4	43.7	40.0	40.3
Netherlands	P/Y	45.8	44.2	36.8	35.8	35.7

Source: Hill [*1979*].

Notes: P = Gross operating surplus.
           K = Gross capital stock.

As suggested above, these high Japanese profits were not the outcome of spontaneous market forces but rather arose in important part from heavy state intervention in the economy. The government had two main proximate objectives: to attain a current account equilibrium at as high a growth rate as possible; to increase the private sector's propensities to invest and save so as to substantially raise the long-term growth rate of the economy.[3] It sought to achieve these objectives by building up the strength and capabilities of Japanese corporations so that these could compete with their counterparts from advanced countries in the international market place. For this purpose a number of measures were taken which directly helped increase the resources available for corporate investment. These were coupled with a range of indirect policies which affected positively the external environment of the corporate sector and thereby also helped raise profits. Each of these sets of measures are briefly outlined below.

The direct policy instruments comprised, *inter alia*, a variety of fiscal incentives to promote corporate growth. Initially, in the early 1950s, these included accelerated depreciation for important industrial equipment, a special deduction for export earnings, a tax free reserve for losses from export transactions, and reduced tax rates on interest and dividends. Over the next two decades, an extraordinary range of other tax concessions were added to this list. There were more than 25 tax-free reserves which were available to corporations by 1975 including those for bad debt, for loss on returned goods unsold, for price fluctuations, for overseas market development, and for overseas investment loss.[4]

(2) Profits and External Environment for the Japanese Corporation

Domestic and external competition: During 1950–73 the Japanese economy operated under generally weak and often unenforced competition laws. There were several reasons for this. First, although the old pre-war *zaibatsu* had been disbanded by the US occupation authorities, the change in the international political climate as a result of the Korean war enabled business firms to regroup again under looser structures called *kieretsu*. Secondly, and more importantly, the anti-trust laws which the US authorities had instituted, did not have a political constituency in post-war Japan and were regarded as a foreign imposition [*Caves and Uekusa, 1976*]. Therefore, after the end of the occupation in 1955, these laws were aggressively undermined by MITI, whose approach came to dominate Japanese economic management. Certainly during this period, MITI had much the upper hand compared with the Japanese Fair Trade Commission, the agency responsible for the enforcement of competition laws.

MITI's basic philosophical approach to 'competition', was rather different from that of the US economists. It did not regard competition *per se* as an end in itself but as a way of promoting technical progress and rapid industrialisation in Japan [*Okimoto, 1989*]. It was therefore as wary of too much competition as it was of too little competition. In order to enhance the competitive capabilities of Japanese firms in the international marketplace, an important objective of MITI was to raise and maintain at high levels the corporate propensity to invest. Too much competition, it felt, could lead to price wars and reduced profits and ultimately lower the inducement to invest.

In line with this analysis, under MITI's sponsorship a wide variety of cartel arrangements were organised, including recession cartels, rationalisation cartels, and so on. According to Caves and Uekusa [*1976*], in the 1960s, cartels accounted for 78.1 per cent of the value of shipments in textiles; 64.8 per cent in clothing; 50.0 per cent in non-ferrous metals; 47 per cent in printing and publishing; 41.2 per cent in stone, clay and glass; 34.5 per cent in steel products, and 37.2 per cent in food products. Although these cartels functioned for only limited periods of time and there was wide variation in their effectiveness, Caves and Uekusa observed that 'their mere presence in such broad stretches of the manufacturing sector attests to their importance' [*Caves and Uekusa, 1976: 147*].

However, as against these instances of MITI's anti-competitive bias, it is also important to note that the Ministry encouraged vigorous competition between large firms in leading industries. It is a moot point whether this was a well-thought out institutional innovation which came from the MITI bureaucracy or whether it was the fact that there were powerful firms in each industry and MITI simply had to accommodate them [*Boltho, 1985*]. Be that as it may, MITI used the extant oligopolistic structure of Japanese industry to promote competition for market share among leading firms. In this respect MITI's approach differed markedly from that of other dirigiste governments, which generally supported a single national champion in each favoured industry.[5]

In Japan, the government through MITI effectively orchestrated 'investment races' among oligopolistic firms. However, to ensure that this did not lead to over-investment, it used 'administrative guidance' to oblige firms to take their turns in carrying out investments. In economic terms, in the real world of incomplete markets, the government provided the crucial coordinating mechanism to ensure market efficiency and continued high rates of investment.

To complement the internal regulation of competition, there were also important restrictions on external competition. Although the formal restrictions on imports were gradually removed from the mid-1960s onwards on the Japanese accession to the OECD, as late as 1978, manufactured imports were only 2.3 per cent of GDP.[6] The corresponding figures for countries like Germany or the United Kingdom were five or six times as large. As Yamamura [*1988*] points out, these restrictions on internal and external competition, instead of being a disadvantage, gave a competitive edge to Japanese firms in the world market. It enabled them to earn high profits in the domestic market, which provided a cushion for their aggressive pursuit of market share in the international markets. MITI, unlike now, during this earlier period had very considerable coercive powers because of its control over foreign exchange allocations. It used these powers to create an incentive structure for Japanese firms to capture world markets. As Singh [*1995e*] notes, companies recognised that to move forward, to have access to foreign exchange, foreign technology, licences, etc., they had to export.

Macroeconomic environment: Another important feature of the external environment faced by Japanese firms during this period was the government's low interest rate policy. This policy helped both to increase the resources available to firms for investment as well as to enhance their willingness to invest. The government practised 'financial repression', that is, it kept the interest rate structure more or less stable at relatively low levels. In effect, this amounted to credit rationing at the discretion of the Bank of Japan and other banks under the so-called 'window guidance' of the Bank of Japan. Credit rationing and low interest rates were also used to subsidise specific industries favoured by the government.

Table 4, on corporate leverage in Japan, the United States and Germany, shows that in terms of book value of assets the Japanese firms during the relevant period were the most highly geared. There is considerable literature on the accuracy of such measurements in view of the very conservative accounting methods used in Japan to record value of land and fixed assets. Nevertheless, even when adjustments are made for the difference in accounting conventions, Japanese firms during the high growth period were still found to be more highly geared than those in either the United States or Germany [*Borio, 1990*].

TABLE 4
CAPITAL STRUCTURE: DEBT EQUITY RATIO OF MANUFACTURING
FIRMS IN GERMANY, JAPAN AND THE UNITED STATES
(Five-year average – Percentage)

	1960–64	1965–69	1970–74
Germany	139.48	152.84	196.94
Japan	236.36	309.91	409.74
United States	55.76	73.45	88.24

Source: Kojima [*1995*].

In view of these high gearing levels of Japanese corporations, the importance of the Japanese government's low interest rate policy cannot be exaggerated. However, leaving aside the question of credit rationing and interest subsidies, in macroeconomic terms, a low interest rate policy could only be sustained if there was an adequate supply of savings, a point taken up below.

(3) Profits and Savings

It was seen earlier that not only Japanese aggregate savings ratios were high by international standards but that each sector of the Japanese economy – households, corporations as well as the government – saved more than its counterparts in most other countries. The high saving propensity of the Japanese corporate sector can be attributed to high profits and high inducement to invest. It was also in part due to the particular feature of the Japanese financial system which permitted companies to follow a policy of low dividend payouts. This issue will be taken up further in the next section.

However, Akyüz and Gore [*1996*] point out that the high savings propensity of the Japanese household sector can also be attributed in part to high levels of profits in the Japanese economy. This is for two reasons. First, the household sector includes unincorporated enterprises; the incomes of these enterprises depend on profits and their savings propensities tend to be high. Secondly, bonus payments to workers which constituted almost a quarter of their annual incomes were also basically a function of profits. Again, the propensity to save out of these bonus payments – which many workers particularly during this period regarded as windfall payments – is estimated to have been quite high (see further Akyüz and Gore [*1996*]).

There are of course a whole host of other explanations for the high savings propensities of the Japanese household sector. These include the fast rate of growth of household incomes, the age and employment structures of the population, the lack of publicly provided social security [*Horioka, 1995*]. Low income elasticity of demand for foreign goods, the low level of development of financing and credit facilities for consumers, formal and informal controls on imports of consumer durables can also be expected to have played a significant part in keeping household consumption low [*UNCTAD, 1997*].

(4) The UNCTAD Thesis: An Initial Assessment

UNCTAD economists have emphasised the central role of profits in the accumulation process in East Asian countries. They observe that profits provide both the funds as well as the incentive for investment, and are also an outcome of investment. Although the observed high profits, high savings and high investments in Japan during the high growth period are generally compatible with this formulation, there is an important difficulty. The foregoing analysis has been conducted entirely in macroeconomic terms, whereas the UNCTAD thesis suggests at least in part microeconomic causality.

The empirical assessment of UNCTAD propositions in relation to Japan is, therefore, incomplete without an analyses of the accumulation process in microeconomic terms. For this purpose, Table 5 presents information on corporate profitability and profit margins in Japan, the United States and Germany. The data indicate that contrary to the findings of the national accounts statistics on the aggregate share of profits in GDP as well as profit rates on aggregate capital stock, both the rates of return and the profit margins of Japanese firms, although not that much different from those of German firms, have been much lower than those of US firms. The observed differences in the corporate rates of return in the United States and Japan can in principle arise from differences in accounting conventions, taxes, etc. However, detailed analysis shows that, even allowing for these factors, Japanese firms in most industries have lower operating margins and returns on assets than the corresponding US firms.[7]

TABLE 5
PROFITABILITY OF MANUFACTURING FIRMS IN
GERMANY, JAPAN AND THE UNITED STATES
(Five-year average, 1960–74 – Percentage)

	Year	Germany	Japan	USA
Return on assets	1960–64	3.00	3.19	6.28
	1965–69	3.07	3.31	6.94
	1970–74	1.87	2.60	5.92
Return on sales	1970–74	1.49	2.94	4.53

Source: Kojima [*1995*].

That the Japanese rates of return are lower than those of the United States at the microeconomic level is not necessarily inconsistent with the much higher Japanese share of profit in the national income relative to the United States. Indeed many economists regard it as a virtue of the Japanese financial system which allows Japanese firms to continue to survive and to invest even when their rates of return are very low. A lower threshold rate of return allows Japanese managers to undertake investments that US firms would find unacceptable. To the extent that a higher rate of investment allows faster turnover of capital equipment and hence greater technical progress and new product development, it gives the Japanese firms a competitive edge over the American corporations.

Indeed in the United States, the MITI Commission on Industrial Productivity [*1989*] regarded this factor as a major reason why US firms lost out to the Japanese corporations in the US home market in a wide range of electronic products. The Commission's investigations showed that when a Japanese firm entered one of these markets, there was a fall in the rate of return of the existing US firms in the industry due to greater competition. This often resulted in the US firms leaving that industry fairly quickly and diversifying and investing their resources elsewhere since they could not accept lower returns. Japanese companies were, however, able to sustain these low rates of return for long periods.

International survey data repeatedly show that Japanese corporate managers are much more interested in pursuing market share than earning a high rate of return on assets or increasing the wealth of the shareholders [*Abegglen and Stalk, 1985*]. This is in sharp contrast to US managers, who the same survey data show accord top priority to shareholder wealth maximisation. These studies of comparative managerial objectives raise two important sets of issues.

(1)   Why do Japanese managers give top priority to the growth of market share?

(2)   Why are they able to ignore shareholder interests?

These issues require an examination of the internal organisation of the Japanese corporation and the relationship between the corporation and the financial system.

In answer to the first question, Odagiri [*1994*] provides persuasive analysis and evidence to suggest that the internal organisation of the Japanese firms obliges the managers to pursue growth maximisation rather than shareholder interests. Even in other advanced countries, such as the United States and the United Kingdom, where there is a separation of ownership from control, non-neoclassical theorists of the firm [*Marris, 1964; Baumol, 1962*] have argued that managers in large corporations are prone to pursue growth maximisation at the expense of firm profitability, that is, they sacrifice profits to growth. Odagiri suggests that because in Japanese firms there is a close relationship between workers and managers, and both identify with the corporation, Japanese managers are likely to exhibit this behaviour even more strongly than US and UK managers. As most Japanese workers and managers in leading firms tend to spend the whole of their working lives in the same corporation, their chances of getting high rewards lie entirely with achieving promotion within the corporation. The more the firm grows, the greater are the opportunities for everyone in the firm to benefit both in terms of job security and in attaining higher-level jobs. Odagiri goes on to argue that it is for the same reason that, unlike US and UK managers in management-controlled corporations,

Japanese managers seek organic growth of the corporation in the same or similar industries rather than growth by takeover in diverse industries. (Such organic growth is more conducive to enhancing job and promotion opportunities than growth by takeovers; besides, takeovers are likely to be opposed by the workers of the victim firms.)

Turning to the question of the ability of Japanese managers to pursue non-shareholder wealth-maximising goals, there are two main factors which are relevant. The first is that Japanese corporations are not subject to the ever present takeover threat of the kind which firms in the United States and the United Kingdom have to endure. Secondly, they have long-term and close relationships (as opposed to 'arms-length' dealings) with their 'parent' banks.

The reasons behind these reasons lie in certain important characteristics of the Japanese financial system. In sharp contrast to the situation in the United States and the United Kingdom, there are hardly any hostile takeovers in Japan. A main reason for this phenomenon is the pattern of share ownership in the typical large Japanese corporate groups. Generally speaking, three-quarters of the shares in such a corporation are likely to be held by suppliers, customers and the lead bank. In other words, there is a concentration of share ownership in a relatively small number of 'safe' hands. Only a quarter of the outstanding shares are traded on the market, which makes it almost impossible to mount a successful hostile takeover. The independent shareholders are obliged to defer to the far larger holdings of the corporation's stakeholders (see further Abegglen and Stalk [1985]; Odagiri [1994]).

There is evidence that the Japanese government, after the Second World War, deliberately encouraged in that country a bank-based rather than a stock-market-based system. The government prevented the growth of the securities market by making among other things: (a) securities unattractive for ordinary savers, (b) restricting residents' and non-residents' access to Japanese securities markets and Japanese access to foreign securities markets, and (c) providing the finance and funds required by the deficit corporate sector through the banking system [Patrick, 1994]. From a sociological perspective, Dore [1985] suggests that in Japan not only is the stock market viewed with suspicion by the general public, it also has a rather inferior social status. It is the government or the real wealth-creating corporate sector which attracts the best talent rather than the stock market.

Thus a typical large Japanese corporation is much less subject to the 'short-termism' which is inherent in the Anglo-Saxon stock market economies.[8] The Japanese firm is regulated by internal group mechanisms, where the group bank plays a critical role. There are sound analytical reasons, as well as empirical evidence, for the view that this kind of bank-based regulation is more conducive to long-term investment not only in plant and equipment, but more importantly in training and in firm-specific, often intangible, human capital.[9]

To sum up, the low observed corporate rates of return in Japan do not necessarily contradict the UNCTAD thesis. Rather, an examination of the nature of the Japanese corporation, characteristic features of the country's financial system and the relationship between the two help to provide a more complete and nuanced analysis. If the internal organisation of the Japanese firms encourages their managers to seek growth of market share at the expense of profits, there will be high corporate investment, low profit rates at the microeconomic level, as well as a high share of profits in national income. It is interesting to note that the same result also follows from the standard neoclassical theory of the profit maximising firm. If the cost of capital is low in Japan because of the high Japanese saving propensity (arising from exogenous factors), a profit maximising firm will expand up to the point where its profitability is equal to the cost of capital, thus resulting in low profit rates, high investment rates and most likely also a high share of profits in national income. The causal mechanism in the two analyses are, however, rather different. Unlike the UNCTAD formulation, whose origins lie in classical economic theory, the neoclassical analysis treats savings as an exogenous rather than an endogenous variable. It also assumes that there are adequate levels of animal spirits among entrepreneurs which would lead to the equilibrium level of investment.

The above analysis also bears on another apparent paradox in relation to the UNCTAD thesis. The paradox arises from the fact that despite the very high gross profits and gross corporate savings as a proportion of GDP in Japan, Japanese companies resort much more to external finance for meeting their investment needs than firms in other countries [*Kojima, 1995*]. There fortunately is a simple explanation for this: Japanese firms use more of both internal and external resources to finance their investments since their growth rates, and hence their need for investment, have been much greater than those of firms in countries such as the United States, Germany and the United Kingdom.

IV. THE GOVERNMENT AND THE CORPORATION IN KOREA

The Korean story of successful industrialisation in the last three decades is intimately linked with the development and the success of the giant Korean corporations, the *chaebols*. These are the large, highly diversified, indeed 'idiosyncratic',[10] conglomerates that have dominated the Korean economy during this period of extraordinarily fast economic growth. The Koreans have also followed a vigorous Japanese-type industrial policy – if anything, the policy has been even more interventionist than in Japan. It has also been marked by a close relationship between the government and business. However, the nature of this relationship in Korea has been somewhat different than that in Japan. Thus, although there are broad similarities, there are also important differences between Japan and Korea with respect to (a) the organisation, ownership patterns and governance of the conglomerates in the two countries; (b) the respective financial systems; and (c) the industrial strategies. The discussion below will attempt to highlight the differences.

The extraordinary economic achievement of Korea during the three decades 1960 to 1990 is encapsulated by the following descriptive statistics. As a consequence of the GNP growing at a sustained rate of ten per cent per annum (and GNP per capita at a rate of nine per cent per annum) over these three decades, the country's per capita GNP rose from just about $300 (at constant 1985 US dollars) in 1962, to well over $5000 in 1991. These changes have been accompanied by radical structural transformations in the economy. The share of manufacturing in output and employment rose to well over 25 per cent in the early 1990s, compared with just ten per cent in 1962. Moreover, in the early 1990s, the country was investing almost 40 per cent of its GDP and the domestic savings rate had increased from 3.2 per cent in 1962 to 36.2 per cent in 1990. The US dollar value of commodity exports increased at an annual average rate of well over 25 per cent per annum over these three decades. Real wages rose on average at a rate of 7.6 per cent per annum. Arguably, the only possible blemish in this exemplary economic record is the relatively high rate of inflation, which averaged more than ten per cent per annum over the whole period; indeed, in the 1970s, the rate of inflation was nearly 20 per cent per annum.[11]

(1) Conglomerate Organisation and the Financial System in Korea

The Korean industrialisation and catching up with advanced countries started in earnest in the early 1960s with the military coup by General Park Chung-Hee (later the President). Park made economic development the top priority of his regime. After an initial period of tension between the government and business, Park came to the view that the large private conglomerate businesses were to be the main vehicles for Korea's catch-up. However, in order for these enterprises to serve the social good, it was necessary for the state to co-ordinate, guide and supervise their actions.[12]

The government of Korea in its support of private business went one step further than in Japan. It actively helped create large conglomerates, promoting mergers and directing entry and exit of firms, according to the requirements of technological-scale economies and world-demand conditions. The result is that the manufacturing industry of the country displays one of the highest levels of market concentration anywhere – whether among the developing or the developed economies. The top 50 *chaebols* accounted for 15 per cent of GDP in 1990. Among the largest 500 industrial companies in the world in 1990, there were 11 firms from the Republic of Korea – the same number as from Switzerland. UN [*1993*] rightly observes in relation to the industrial structure of Korea: 'Such a structure is the deliberate creation of the government, which utilised a highly interventionist strategy to push industry into larger-scale, complex technologically demanding activities while simultaneously restricting FDI inflows tightly to promote national ownership'.

There are some important differences between the Korean *chaebols* and the Japanese *kieretsu*. In the Japanese *kieretsu*, there is a sharp divorce of ownership from control. Although, as noted earlier, nearly three-quarters of the shares in a *kieretsu* member firm may be held in 'patient' hands of other stakeholders, there is, nevertheless, very little family share ownership and control. In contrast, the Korean *chaebols* are to a considerable extent family-owned and controlled. The absence of family ownership means that the Japanese corporations are effectively run by professional managers. The *chaebols*, however, are run by the founding families, who take the top management positions, rather than by professional managers.[13]

The second crucial organisational difference between the *chaebols* and the *kieretsus* derives from the important differences in the financial systems of the two countries. The Korean financial system during the high growth period was effectively under state control so that the relationship between the main bank and the 'group' firms in Korea has been rather different from that in Japan. In Japan, the group's main bank may be subject to government persuasion through 'window guidance', etc., by the Bank of Japan, but it is nevertheless a private entity. When the main bank is directly state-owned and controlled as in Korea for much of the period, the relationship between the bank and the firms in the group becomes rather different. The state-owned bank provides the government with an additional layer of control as well as information about the group's activities. Lee [*1992*] has argued, in defence of this kind of relationship between the financial system and the corporate organisation, that the government and large private organisations together can be regarded as forming an internal organisation. The relationship between the financial system and the corporations can therefore be conceptualised as an internal capital market. Following Williamson [*1975*], Lee suggests that such a financial system is not necessarily inefficient and can indeed be more useful than a free market financial system which suffers from various market imperfections.

(2) Industrial Strategy

After a period of import substitution industrialisation in the 1950s and 1960s, the Korean government embarked in the second half of the latter decade on a purposive strategy of promoting exports, whilst maintaining extensive protection of its own markets. An essential purpose of this policy was to attain a current account equilibrium at as high a long-term growth rate of the economy as possible. This task was more difficult for Korea than for Japan for two reasons. First, Japan was relatively more developed than Korea. Secondly, Japan had a much larger internal market. Importantly, Japanese economic growth during the high growth period was not export-led. The share of exports in GDP increased only to a small degree in the two decades 1953 to 1973, from 6.5 per cent in 1953 to 8.9 per cent in 1973. Korean industrialisation on the other hand was definitely export-led. In the comparable period of high growth in Korea, its exports increased from 4.8 per cent of GDP in 1963 to 34.0 per cent in 1980 [*Krueger, 1995*].

To achieve such export-led growth required stronger government involvement in building up the capabilities of private corporations to compete in the international market. The government did this by a wide rage of measures which helped the corporate sector to invest and to improve its technological development, as well as have the resources to finance these investment projects. Some of the policies adopted by the government for these purposes are elaborated below.

(3) Domestic and External Competition

The Korean economy was characterised by a high and growing degree of industrial concentration during its high growth phase. Normally, fast economic growth leads to reduced industrial concentration as it allows entry and expansion of new firms. However, during the 1970s and until the mid-1980s, this pattern was not observed in Korea. Most of the economic expansion came from the growth of existing firms and their subsidiaries; the contribution of new enterprises was very small. Korea's all-industry average three-firm concentration ratio in the early 1980s was higher than Japan's – 62 per cent compared with 56.3 per cent [*Lee and Lee, 1990*]. Between 1970 and 1982 the share of total manufacturing shipments produced under a competitive market structure in Korea decreased from roughly 40 per cent to 30 per cent, while the share produced by oligopolies increased from 35 per cent to 50 per cent [*Lee and Lee, 1990*]. By 1987, however, the share of shipments produced under competitive market conditions did, in fact, rise to 43 per cent, while the share accounted for by oligopolies fell to 40 per cent [*Lee and Lee, 1990*]. This rise of competition cannot, however, be attributed to anti-monopoly legislation, which was introduced in the 1980s but which was implemented only weakly and sporadically. Thus, rapid economic growth in Korea did ultimately lead to declining industry concentration, but it took much longer to materialise than elsewhere [*Amsden and Singh, 1994*].

Notwithstanding the high degree of industrial concentration, there was nevertheless fierce competition among the large conglomerate groups [*Kim, 1992*]. The Korean government went out of its way to ensure that big business did not collude, by allocating subsidies only in exchange for strict performance standards [*Amsden, 1989*]. After 1975 inter-group competition became even more intense as each *chaebol* tried to qualify for generous subsidies to establish a general trading company by meeting government performance standards regarding minimum export volume and number of export products [*Cho, 1987*].

Amsden and Singh [*1994*] note that although the Korean government disciplined subsidy recipients, it also supported them for lengthy periods until they ultimately became internationally competitive. This enabled firms to have long time horizons for their investment plans. The Korean automobile industry, for example, has been protected from foreign competition for almost three decades. This is despite the fact that the industry has long ceased to be an 'infant' and has indeed emerged as a major exporter. Korea is expected to become the fourth largest car producer in the world by the year 2000. However, in 1995, the country imported only 4,000 cars.

(4) Inducement to Invest and the Socialisation of Risk

As in Japan, the government in Korea played a critical role in enhancing and maintaining at a high level the corporate inducement to invest. However, the state in Korea was not just a referee or a ringmaster in orchestrating investment races, it was also a nursemaid and a fairy godmother to the *chaebols*. During the 1970s when the government implemented its extremely ambitious 'heavy and chemical industry' (HCI) programme, it virtually became a co-partner with the leading *chaebols* and 'socialised' the risks involved. The economic downturn of the early 1970s provides a striking illustration of the Korean government's approach to industrial development.

In view of the high leverage of Korean *chaebols* (see Table 6), the recession, coupled with devaluation and a rise in interest rates, threatened the financial viability of many strategic corporations engaged in HCI. The government responded forcefully with the Presidential Emergency Decree of August 1972, which declared a moratorium on corporate debt to curb market lenders. Kim *et al.* [*1995*] note that all corporate loans from the curb market were converted into long-term loans to be paid on an instalment

basis over a five year period with a grace period of three years. A maximum
interest rate of 16.2 per cent was fixed on these loans while the prevailing
curb market rate was over 40 per cent per annum.

TABLE 6
FINANCIAL INDICATORS IN THE MANUFACTURING
INDUSTRY IN KOREA, 1963–76
(Percentages)

Year	Rate of debt to equity[a]	Ratio of interest expenses to net sales	Ratio of net profits to net sales
1963	92.2	3.0	9.1
1964	100.5	4.9	8.6
1965	83.7	3.9	7.9
1966	117.7	5.7	7.7
1967	151.2	5.2	6.7
1968	201.3	5.9	6.0
1969	270.0	7.8	4.3
1970	328.4	9.2	3.3
1971	394.2	9.9	1.2
1972	313.4	7.1	3.9
1973	272.7	4.6	7.5
1974	316.0	4.5	4.8
1975	339.5	4.9	3.4
1976	364.6	4.9	3.9

Source: Kim *et al.* [*1995*].

Note: a Total liabilities/net worth.

Korea's HCI drive is often criticised by orthodox economists [*World
Bank, 1993; Krueger, 1995*] as an example of inefficiency and waste and
general government failure. However, this assessment is disputed by other
economists who point out that there were inevitable teething troubles with
a highly ambitious programme of this kind designed to fundamentally
transform the structure of the Korean economy. In a long-term view, HCI
can be regarded as being exceptionally valuable as since the mid-1980s it
has been the main source of Korea's outstanding export success in the world
markets [*Amsden, 1989; Kim et al., 1995*]. Moreover, these three authors
also suggest that HCI expanded the spectrum of the product mix in the
economy and provided domestic producers enormous scope for learning by
doing. They believe that the Korean experience confirms the Lucas [*1993*]
hypothesis that the quicker the introduction of new products, the quicker the
process of learning by doing and the faster the overall expansion of the

economy. Kim *et al.* conclude that the government's active risk sharing with private firms made an important contribution to the successful implementation of the HCI programme.

(5) The Financing of Corporate Growth in Korea

Table 7 provides comparative information on the financing of corporate growth for four industrial countries – the United States, the United Kingdom, Germany and Japan – and for Korea. The table is based on aggregate flow of funds accounts and refers to the non-financial corporate sector as a whole. The figures for the industrial countries refers to the period 1970 to 1989 and for Korea for the years 1975 to 1990. There are serious data difficulties in making such international comparisons, but as far as possible a broadly similar methodology has been used for the decomposition of the sources of finance for all five countries in Table 7. It would have perhaps been more useful to compare the Korean pattern of financing corporate growth with that of other semi-industrial countries, but unfortunately the lack of comparable flow of funds data prevents such an exercise.

TABLE 7
GROSS SOURCES OF FINANCE FOR FIVE COUNTRIES

	1970–89				1975–90
	UK	USA	Germany	Japan	Korea
Retentions	60.4	62.7	62.4	40.0	30.0
New equity	7.0	–4.9	2.3	3.9	12.8
Bonds	2.3	12.8	0.9	3.9	12.0
Loans	23.3	14.7	18.0	34.5	29.5
Trade credit	1.9	8.8	1.8	15.6	7.8
Other	5.2	5.9	14.6	2.1	7.9
Total external	39.6	37.3	37.6	60.0	70.0

Source: Cho [*1995*].

Table 7 shows that the Korean pattern of financing of corporate growth is much more similar to that of Japan than that of the other three industrial countries. Korean corporations, however, finance an even smaller proportion of their growth from retained earnings than the Japanese companies. Korean companies also rely to a greater extent on new equity finance than companies in the United Kingdom or the United States, where one might have thought a priori that stock market financing would be more important. The results of Table 7 conform to the conclusions reached by

Singh and Hamid [*1992*] and Singh [*1995d*] that large developing country corporations rely to a far greater extent on (a) external finance, and (b) equity finance than may be expected on theoretical grounds as well as on the basis of the experience of advanced country corporations.

However, as noted earlier in the case of Japan, the greater reliance on external finance by developing country corporations is not difficult to explain: given their much faster growth rates, these corporations need both more internal and external funds to finance their growth. Indeed, Cho [*1995*] reports for Korea a consistent negative relationship between internal finance and loan finance, suggesting that the lower the level of internal finance, the greater the 'need' for companies to finance its investment programme from outside sources. The greater reliance on equity financing of Korean corporations relative to those of advanced countries is, however, a more complex subject, but it is not directly relevant to the purpose of the present analysis.[14]

(6) Profits, Savings and Investment at the Macroeconomic Level

We have seen above that the Korean corporate sector relied heavily on external sources (mainly banks) to finance its growth. It is also clear from the previous discussion that at the microeconomic level, the Korean *chaebols* were not motivated by short-term profitability but rather by their desire to maintain and improve the market share. It will be recalled from section II above that the Japanese firms behaved in a similar way, but the factors which were responsible for inducing such firm motivation were somewhat different in the Japanese case as compared with that of Korean firms. In Korea, the state played a much more overt and visible role in influencing firm motivation and behaviour.

We shall now examine the role of profits in the Korean economy at the macroeconomic level and consider how these might have contributed towards meeting the macroeconomic constraint of the equality of *ex ante* savings and investments at high growth rates. Table 8 provides information on the gross share of profits in gross production as well as aggregate profit rates for the Korean manufacturing industry over the last three decades.

Two important points emerge from Table 8. First, the Korean profit share in the 1960s and the 1970s was quite high – averaging well over 40 per cent in both decades. The figures for both profit share and profit rates for two decades are similar to those of Japan in that country's high growth period. Secondly, we note a trend decline in both profit rates and profit shares in Korea after 1978. Between 1977 and 1987, average profit share declined by at least five percentage points. There appears to have been a further sharper decline since 1987. The lower profit share could be attributed in part to tighter labour market conditions and the rising power of

TABLE 8
MANUFACTURING GROSS PROFIT RATES AND PROFIT SHARE
IN KOREA, 1963–90
(Selected years – Percentages)

	Profit rate	Profit share
1963	29.9	41.6
1965	33.9	45.3
1970	28.8	40.8
1975	25.5	46.2
1978	20.2	35.5
1980	12.8	30.4
1982	13.8	33.6
1985	17.0	38.5
1988	14.0	30.7
1990	12.2	32.5

Source: Jang [*1995*].

the trade union, both in the period leading up to democratisation in the late 1980s as well as subsequently.

Turning specifically to the issue of the investment-profits-savings nexus, the following points are significant. First, the high Korean profits and corporate investments would have contributed directly to raising business savings. Moreover, these profits most likely would also have helped raise savings to some degree in the household sector – for much the same reasons as those for Japan discussed earlier, that is, the inclusion of unincorporated businesses in the household sector as well as bonus payment to workers which constituted 15 per cent of workers' wages during the early 1980s [*UNCTAD, 1997*]. Secondly, the flow-of-funds data indicate that although business savings in Korea were high in comparative international terms, these could finance only 40 per cent of business investment; the rest of the finance had to be mobilised from other sectors. The government actively participated in this mobilisation effort, so as to maintain macroeconomic equilibrium between savings and investments at high growth rates. A broad range of policies to discourage luxury consumption constituted a conspicuous part of the government programme in this area [*Chang, 1997*].

Thirdly, although comparable long time-series information on profits (corresponding to Table 8 for Korea) is not available for other developing countries, UNCTAD [*1997*] has assembled some (admittedly imperfect) data on the subject for a number of developing countries for the most recent period. These data suggest that in comparative terms Korean profit share has not been any larger than that in a number of other developing countries, particularly in Latin America. However, the savings and investment rates of these Latin American countries were considerably lower than Korea's, indicating *inter alia* a low level of animal spirits or a high level of consumption by the entrepreneurial classes, or a combination of the two.

V. CONCLUSION

This study has analysed the relationship between profits, savings and investment in the exemplary East Asian economies both at the microeconomic and macroeconomic levels. It has paid particular attention to (a) the role of the government and government–business interactions; and (b) the relationship between the financial system and the corporation. It has emphasised the significance of these relationships for raising and maintaining at a high level the corporate propensity to invest in East Asian economies.

Although stimulating the 'animal spirits' of the private corporations is an essential step in the accumulation process, it is by no means sufficient. The governments in Korea and Japan also adopted a wide range of policies to ensure that the main macroeconomic constraints on fast economic growth – the equality of *ex ante* savings and investments and current account equilibrium at high growth rates – were achieved. For otherwise the growth and accumulation process will be frustrated with negative consequences for corporate propensity to invest. High corporate and overall profits, in part made possible by deliberate government policies, were crucial in satisfying these macroeconomic constraints.

It will be useful to note that apart from its intellectual interest in its own right, the emphasis in Akyüz *et al.* [*1997*], as well as in the present paper, on the accumulation process in explaining East Asian economic growth, is particularly timely from a present-day policy perspective. This is because, in analytical terms, raising the propensities to save and invest can be regarded as one way of enhancing a country's long-term international competitiveness. It complements the traditional industrial policies of import substitution and export promotion which many developing countries, including the East Asian ones, have normally used for this purpose.[15] However, if under liberalisation and globalisation in the post-Uruguay Round global economic order, the traditional industrial policies have to be phased out, poor countries will necessarily be obliged to focus on savings and investment propensities for achieving macroeconomic equilibria at high growth rates.[16] Finally, in the light of the current financial crisis in East Asian countries, an important question is whether their hitherto highly successful model of capital accumulation outlined in this essay is mainly responsible for the crisis as some suggest. Singh [*1998*] focuses directly on this issue and comes to the conclusion that it was precipitate financial liberalisation and the abandonment of certain features of the traditional East Asian accumulation model in the recent period which were the main causes of the crisis.

NOTES

1. Some [*Young, 1994; Krugman, 1994*] would regard this as the primary factor responsible for fast economic growth in East Asia. Others, such as the World Bank [*1993*], give more weight to the higher total factor productivity growth of these countries relative to others, but nevertheless regard the high savings and investment rates to have been an important factor in accounting for the East Asian economic success. See further Singh [*1995a*].
2. In the absence of readily available data for developing countries, comparative international data for developed countries have been used in this and in some of the following tables.
3. See further Ackley and Ishi [*1976*], Singh [*1995b*], and Singh [*1997*].
4. For analyses of the effects of these fiscal measures, see Ackley and Ishi [*1976*]; Pechman and Kaizuka [*1976*]; see also Tsuru [*1993*].
5. It is this dual nature of competition policies in Japan, whereby competition is encouraged in some industries while it is discouraged in others, which leads some writers to emphasise the competitive aspects of the policy (see, for example, Porter [*1990*]), and others to stress its anti-competitive nature as, for example, Caves and Ukeusa [*1976*]). These partial views of competition policy in Japan do not, however, reflect the unity of purpose in the management of competition by the Japanese authorities, particularly by MITI. See further Amsden and Singh [*1994*].
6. This indicates the significance of the informal import controls in Japan which often arose as a part of Japanese business practice. See further Johnson *et al.* [*1989*].
7. See further Blaine [*1993*]. Blaine has carried out a comprehensive examination of the financial statement ratio of large firms in 13 major industries in the United States and Japan over the period 1985-89. See also Odagiri [*1994*].
8. There is a large literature on the stock market and the short termism that it typically engenders. For a recent review, see Singh [*1995c*]. See also Stein [*1988, 1989*]; Cosh *et al.* [*1992*]; Singh [*1992*]; Porter [*1992*]; Kojima [*1995*]; Froot *et al.* [*1992*]. For an opposite point of view on the subject, see Marsh [*1990*].
9. See further Frank and Mayer [*1990*]; Jacobson and Aaker [*1993*]; Stiglitz [*1993*]; Allen and Gale [*1995*].
10. The phrase is G. Pfeffermann's [*Singh, 1995d*] to indicate the large number of different, technologically unconnected, products that Korean firms typically produce.
11. The source of the statistics in this paragraph is Kim *et al.* [*1995*].
12. Park wrote: 'One of the essential characteristics of a modern economy is its strong tendency towards centralisation. Mammoth enterprise – considered indispensable at the moment to our country – plays not only a decisive role in the economic development and elevation of living standards, but further brings about changes in the structure of society and the economy. ...Therefore, the key problems facing a free economic policy are coordination and supervisory guidance, by the state, of mammoth economic strength' (as cited in Amsden [*1994*]).

13. Professionalisation of management, however, is gradually taking place in many chaebols. See further Amsden [*1989*].
14. This issue is fully examined in Singh [*1995d*].
15. For the East Asian countries, for the classic studies of Korea and Taiwan, see respectively Amsden [*1989*] and Wade [*1990*].
16. For a fuller discussion of this argument see Singh [*1995f, 1996*].

REFERENCES

Abegglen, J.C. and G.C. Stalk, 1985, *The Japanese Corporation*, New York: Basic Books.
Ackley, G. and H. Ishi, 1976, 'Fiscal, Monetary and Related Policies', in Ch.3, H. Patrick and H. Rosovsky (eds.), *Asia's New Giant: How the Japanese Economy Works*, Washington, DC: The Brookings Institute.
Akyüz, Y. and C. Gore, 1996, 'The Investment-Profits Nexus in East Asian Industrialisation', *World Development*, Vol.24, No.3.
Akyüz, Y., H.-J. Chang and R. Kozul-Wright, 1997, 'New Perspectives on East Asian Development', this volume.
Allen, F. and D. Gale, 1995, 'A Welfare Comparison of Intermediaries and Financial Markets in Germany and the US', *European Economic Review*, Vol.39, pp.179–209.
Amsden, A., 1989, *Asia's Next Giant*, New York: Oxford University Press.
Amsden, A., 1994, 'Big-Business-Focused Industrialisation in South Korea', in A.D. Chandler, T. Hikino and F. Amatore (eds.), *Big Business and the Wealth of Nations in the Past Century, 1880s–1980s*, Cambridge: Cambridge University Press.
Amsden, A. and A. Singh, 1994, 'The Optimal Degree of Competition and Dynamic Efficiency in Japan and Korea', *European Economic Review*, Vol.38, No.3/4, April, pp.941–51.
Baumol, W.J., 1962, 'On the Theory of the Expansion of the Firm', *American Economic Review*, Vol.52, No.5, Dec.
Blaine, M., 1993, 'Profitability and Competitiveness: Lessons from Japanese and American Firms in the 1980s', *California Management Review*, Vol.36, Fall, pp.48–74.
Boltho, A., 1975, *Japan: An Economic Survey, 1953-1973*, London: Oxford University Press.
Boltho, A., 1985, 'Was Japan'sIndustrial Policy Successful?', *Cambridge Journal of Economics*, Vol.9, No.2, June.
Borio, C.E.V., 1990, 'Leverage and Financing of Non-Financial Companies: An International Perspective', *BIS Economic Paper*, No.27, Basle: Bank for International Settlements.
Caves, R.E. and M. Uekusa, 1976, *Industrial Organisation in Japan*, Washington, DC: The Brookings Institution.
Chang, H.J., 1997, *The Political Economy of Industrial Policy*, London: St. Martins Press.
Cho, D.S., 1987, *The General Trading Company: Concept and Strategy*, Lexington, MA: Lexington Books.
Cho, Y.D., 1995, 'Financial Factors and Corporate Investment: A Microeconometric Analysis of Korean Manufacturing Firms', Ph.D. dissertation, University of Oxford.
Cosh, A., Hughes, A. and A. Singh, 1992, 'Takeovers and Short-Termism in the UK', *Industrial Policy Paper*, No.3, London: Institute for Public Policy Research.
Dore, R., 1985, 'Financial Structures and the Long-Term View', *Policy Studies*, July.
Frank, J. and C. Mayer, 1990, 'Capital Markets and Corporate Control: A Study of France, Germany and the UK', *Economic Policy*.
Froot, K.A., Perold, A.F. and J.C. Stein, 1992, 'Shareholder Trading Practices and Corporate Investment Horizons', *Journal of Applied Corporate Finance*, Vol.5, Summer, pp.42–58.
Hill, T.P., 1979, *Profits and Rates of Return*, Paris: OECD.
Horioka, C.Y., 1995, 'Is Japan's Household Saving Rate Really High?', *Review of Income and Wealth*, Series 41, No.4, Dec.
Honohan, P. and I. Atiyas, 1993, 'Intersectoral Financial Flows in Developing Countries', *The Economic Journal*, Vol.103, No.419, May, pp.666–79.
Jacobson, R. and D. Aaker, 1993, 'Myopic Management Behaviour with Efficient, but Imperfect, Financial Markets: A Comparison of Information Asymmetries in the US and Japan',

136   EAST ASIAN DEVELOPMENT: NEW PERSPECTIVES

Journal of Accounting and Economics, Vol.16, pp.383–405.

Jang, H., 1995, 'Phases of Capital Accumulation in Korea and Evolution of Government Strategy, 1963–1990', Ph.D. dissertation, University of Oxford.

Johnson, C., Tyson, L. and J. Zysman, 1989, *Politics and Productivity*, New York: Harper Business.

Kim, J.K., Shim, S.D. and J. Kim, 1995, 'The Role of the Government in Promoting Industrialisation and Human Capital Accumulation in Korea', in Takatoshi Ito and Anne Krueger (eds.), *Growth Theories in Light of the East Asian Experience*, Chicago, IL and London: University of Chicago Press.

Kim, M.J., 1992, 'Korea's Successful Economic Development and the World Bank', mimeo.

Kojima, K., 1995, 'An International Perspective on Japanese Corporate Finance', *RIEB Kobe University Discussion Paper*, No.45, March.

Krueger, A.O., 1995, 'East Asian Experience and Endogenous Growth Theory', in Takatoshi Ito and Anne Krueger (eds.), *Growth Theories in Light of the East Asian Experience*, Chicago, IL and London: University of Chicago Press.

Krugman, P., 1994, 'The Myth of Asia's Miracle', *Foreign Affairs*, Vol.73, No.6, Nov./Dec.

Lee, C.H., 1992, 'The Government, Financial System and Large Private Enterprises in Economic Development of South Korea, *World Development*, Vol.20, No.2, pp.187–97.

Lee, K. and J. Lee, 1990, *Business Groups and Economic Concentration in Korea*, Seoul: Korea Development Institute.

Lucas, R.E, 1993, 'Making a Miracle', *Econometrica*, Vol.61, pp.251–72.

Marris, R.L., 1964, *The Economic Theory of 'Managerial' Capitalism*, London: Macmillan.

Marsh, P., 1990, *Short-termism on Trial*, London: Institutional Fund Managers Association.

MITI Commission on Industrial Productivity, 1989, *Made in America: Regaining the Productivity Edge*, Cambridge, MA: MIT Press.

Odagiri, H., 1994, *Growth Through Competition, Competition Through Growth*, Oxford: Clarendon Press.

Okimoto, D.I, 1989, *Between the MITI and the Market*, Palo Alto, CA: Stanford University Press.

Patrick, H., 1994, 'The Relevance of Japanese Finance and its Main Bank System', in M. Aoki and H. Patrick (eds.), *The Japanese Main Bank System: Its Relevance for Developing and Transforming Economies*, Oxford: Oxford University Press.

Pechman, J.A. and K. Kaizuka, 1976, 'Taxation', in H. Patrick and H. Rosovsky (eds.), *Asia's New Giant: How the Japanese Economy Works,* Washington, DC: The Brookings Institute.

Porter, M.E., 1990, *The Competitive Advantage of Nations*, London: Macmillan Press.

Porter, M.E., 1992, 'Capital Disadvantage: America's Failing Capital Investment System', *Harvard Business Review,* Sept.–Oct., pp.65–82.

Singh, A., 1992, 'Corporate Takeovers', in J. Eatwell, M. Milgate and P. Newman (eds.), *The New Palgrave Dictionary of Money and Finance*, London: Macmillan.

Singh, A., 1995a, 'The Causes of Fast Economic Growth in East Asia', *UNCTAD Review 1995*, Geneva, pp.91–127.

Singh, A., 1995b, 'Competitive Markets and Economic Development: A Commentary on World Bank Analyses', *International Papers in Political Economy*, Vol.2, No.1.

Singh, A., 1995c, 'The Anglo-Saxon Market for Corporate Control, the Financial System and International Competitiveness', *Working Paper*, No.AF16, March. Department of Applied Economics, Finance and Accounting, University of Cambridge.

Singh, A., 1995d, *Corporate Financing Patterns in Industrialising Economies: A Comparative International Study,* IFC Technical Paper, No.1, Washington, DC: World Bank.

Singh, A., 1995e, 'The Causes of Fast Economic Growth in East Asia', *UNCTAD Review 1995*, Geneva.

Singh, A., 1995f, 'The Post-Uruguay Round World Trading System, Industrialisation, Trade and Development', in UNCTAD, *Expansion of Trading Opportunities to the Year 2000 for Asia-Pacific Developing Countries*, Geneva: UNCTAD.

Singh, A., 1996, 'Savings, Investment and the Corporation in the East Asian Miracle', *Study No.9*, Geneva: UNCTAD.

Singh, A., 1997, 'Catching Up with the West: A Perspective on Asian Economic Development and Lessons for Latin America', in Louis Emmerij, *Economic and Social Development into the XXI Century,* Inter-American Development Bank.

Singh, A., 1998, 'The Asian Capitalism and the Financial Crisis', paper presented at the Conference on Global Instability and World Economic Governance held in May 1998, Robinson College, Cambridge; forthcoming in J. Michie and J.G. Smith, *Global Instability and World Economic Governance,* Oxford: Oxford University Press.

Singh, A. and J. Hamid, 1992, *Corporate Financial Structures in Developing Countries,* IFC Technical Paper, No.1, Washington, DC: World Bank.

Stein, J., 1988, 'Takeover Threat and Managerial Myopia', *Journal of Political Economy,* Vol.96, pp.61–80.

Stein, J., 1988/89, 'Efficient Capital Markets, Inefficient Firms: A Model of Myopic Corporate Behaviour', *Quarterly Journal of Economics,* Vol.104, pp.655–69.

Stiglitz, J.E., 1993, 'The Role of the State in Financial Markets', *Proceedings of the World Bank Annual Conference on Development Economics,* Washington, DC: The World Bank.

Tsuru, S., 1993, *Japan Capitalism: Creative Defeat and Beyond,* Cambridge: Cambridge University Press.

UN, 1993, *Transnational Corporations from Developing Countries,* New York: United Nations.

UNCTAD, 1997, *Trade and Development Report,* Geneva and New York: United Nations.

Wade, R., 1990, *Governing the Market,* Princeton, NJ: Princeton University Press.

Williamson, O.E., 1975, *Markets and Hierarchies: Analysis and Antitrust Implications,* New York: The Free Press.

World Bank, 1993, *The East Asian Miracle: Economic Growth and Public Policy,* New York: Oxford University Press for the World Bank.

Yamamura, K., 1988, 'Caveat Emptor': The Industrial Policy of Japan', in P. Krugman (ed.), Strategic Trade Policy and the New International Economics, Cambridge, MA: The MIT Press.

Young, A., 1994, 'Lessons from the East Asian NICs: A Contrarian View', *European Economic Review,* Vol.38, No.3/4, April.

Index

agreements 30
trade related investment measures (TRIMs)
  30
trade unionism 54, 132
training 14, 19, 21, 26, 124
transferable lessons 66, 69, 78–83
transnational corporations (TNCs), exports
  and 21, 32
  gains from hosting 27
  industralisation and 15
  Japanese 23
  Singapore and 75
transportation 21
'trickle-down' thesis 45
Tunisia 40, 50
Turkey 50

Uekusa, M. 117–18
UNCTAD, (1992) 13
  (1994) 17
  (1996) 9, 15, 30, 69, 73, 81
  (1997) 37, 52, 120, 132, 133
UNCTAD research 1, 3–4
United Kingdom 3, 40, 114–16, 118, 122–4,
  130
  sectoral savings and investment 49–50
  wage differential 57–8
United States, aid to Korea 100, 108
  aid to Taiwan 91, 94, 97, 99
  anti-trust laws 117
  corporate leverage in 119
  corporate profitability and profit margins
    121
  FDI in China and ASEAN 24
  Gini coefficient for wealth distribution 56
  gross fixed investment ratios (1953–72)
    114
  gross profits and rates of return 115–16
  gross sources of finance 130

income inequality 40
investment rates 124
separation of ownership from control in
  firms 122
takeover threats 123
wages 57–8
Uruguay Round 30–31, 133

Venezuela 40, 58
Viet Nam 21–2
virtuous circle, income distribution and
  human capital accumulation 55

Wade, Robert 67, 72, 76, 88, 90, 92, 95, 98
wage-earning opportunities 51, 58, 62
waiting strategies, long-term investment
  commitments and 8
Wang, L.S. 94, 97, 99
'Weberian bureaucracy' 70–71, 80
Western countries, income distribution 43
'window guidance', Bank of Japan and 119,
  126
Wolf, C. 100, 102
wood 13
worker remittances, foreign exchange and 10
World Bank 5, 42–3, 45, 59
World Bank, (1987) 46
  (1993) 5, 7, 16, 38, 45, 54, 58, 129
  (1994) 39
  (1995) 45
World Development Report (1994) 51
World Trade Organisation (WTO) 30–32, 81

yen appreciation (1985) 23
You, Jong-Il 11, 17, 37, 46
Yuan 73, 94, 95, 99

zaibatsu 46, 117

Titles of Related Interest

THE STATE AND ECONOMIC DEVELOPMENT
Lessons from the Far East

Robert Fitzgerald, *Royal Holloway, University of London (Ed)*

This book explores the role of national governments during the process of industrialisation in East Asia and examines the relationship between the State and business, clearing up many Western misconceptions. The similarities and differences which exist between nations in this region and the influence of Japan as a role model are also investigated. Government-industry linkages and an overview of economic rationale also studied in this volume are following the establishment of market orientated economies in many Far Eastern countries. This book brings new insight into the business-politics relationship which gives the reader a complete understanding of the East Asian economic 'miracle'.

160 pages   1995
0 7146 4638 5 cloth
0 7146 4159 6 paper
A special issue of the journal Asia Pacific Business Review

FRANK CASS PUBLSHERS
Newbury House, 900 Eastern Avenue, Newbury Park, Ilford, Essex, IG2 7HH
Tel: +44 (0)181 599 8866 Fax: +44 (0)181 599 0984

NORTH AMERICA
c/o ISBS, 5804 NE Hassalo Street, Portland OR 97213 3644
Tel: (800) 944 6190 Fax: (503) 280 8832 E-mail: orders@isbs.com

Website: http://www.frankcass.com E-mail: sales@frankcass.com

SYSTEMIC COMPETITIVENESS
New Governance Patterns for Industrial Development

Klaus Esser, Wolfgang Hillebrand, Dirk Messner *and*
Jörg Meyer-Stamer, *all at the German Development Institute*

Enhancing competitiveness poses a key challenge to all countries. The analysis of different developing regions shows that the most dynamic countries are not those that bank solely on competition between isolated firms, unconditioned free trade and the state as an institution of regulation and supervision. Instead the successful countries are those that actively shape locational and competitive advantages. The authors emphasise that an economy's competitiveness rests on purposive and intermeshed measures at four system levels (the meta-, macro-, meso- and micro-levels), and a multidimensional guidance concept consisting of competition, dialogue and shared decision-making, which integrates the key groups of actors.

172 pages   1996
0 7146 4251 7 paper
GDI Book Series No 7

FRANK CASS PUBLSHERS
Newbury House, 900 Eastern Avenue, Newbury Park, Ilford, Essex, IG2 7HH
Tel: +44 (0)181 599 8866 Fax: +44 (0)181 599 0984

NORTH AMERICA
c/o ISBS, 5804 NE Hassalo Street, Portland OR 97213 3644
Tel: (800) 944 6190 Fax: (503) 280 8832 E-mail: orders@isbs.com

Website: http://www.frankcass.com E-mail: sales@frankcass.com

THE ECONOMICS OF GROUNDWATER MANAGEMENT IN ARID COUNTRIES
Theory, International Experience and a Case Study of Jordan

Manuel Schiffler, *German Development Institute*

Groundwater is being depleted on a large scale in many arid and semi-arid parts of the world. It is often said that this precious resource is being wasted at the expense of future generations. But should ground-water depletion be avoided at any price? Or is depletion desirable in certain circumstances? If there is to be a reduction in groundwater depletion, how can it be achieved? And how can limited water resources be allocated to their most valuable uses?

The author addresses these issues by undertaking an economic analysis, and considers the political and hydrological aspects of water management. Various methods of assessing the economic value of water are presented, a hydroeconomic model is developed to enable the economic value of groundwater stocks in different circumstances to be estimated, and a framework for the analysis of agricultural–urban water transfers is introduced. Eight types of groundwater management policy instruments are discussed on the basis of both theory and international experience.

432 pages   1998
0 7146 4907 4 cloth
0 7146 4457 9 paper
GDI Book Series No 11

FRANK CASS PUBLSHERS
Newbury House, 900 Eastern Avenue, Newbury Park, Ilford, Essex, IG2 7HH
Tel: +44 (0)181 599 8866 Fax: +44 (0)181 599 0984

NORTH AMERICA
c/o ISBS, 5804 NE Hassalo Street, Portland OR 97213 3644
Tel: (800) 944 6190 Fax: (503) 280 8832 E-mail: orders@isbs.com

Website: http://www.frankcass.com E-mail: sales@frankcass.com

THE NETWORK SOCIETY
Economic Development and International
Competitiveness as Problems of Social Governance

Dirk Messner, *Institute for Development and Peace,*
Duisburg

The globalization of the economy has become an irreversible,
universally dominant trend. Industrialized and developing nations
as well as countries in transformation have to face the challenge of
building internationally competitive economic structures. One-
sidedly liberalist economic policies do not lead to the emergence
of 'systemic competitiveness'. What is called for are active
development strategies. But how are they to be implemented, and
what is the state of the political governance capacity of societies in
the context of the new world economy?

The author argues that the countries that will, at the end of the
twentieth century, meet with the greatest economic, social, and
ecological success will not be unleashed market economies but
'active and learning societies' that attempt to solve their problems
on the basis of an organizational and governance-related pluralism.
The book analyses its contours, functional logics, as well as
creativity and blockade potentials. The narrow sets of categories
offered by traditional theories of the market and the state are not
adequate to the task of depicting the far-reaching institutional-
organizational processes of change facing modern and modernizing
societies and economies. The book unfolds the picture of the
'network society'.

416 pages   1997
0 7146 4402 1 paper
GDI Book Series No 10

FRANK CASS PUBLSHERS
Newbury House, 900 Eastern Avenue, Newbury Park, Ilford, Essex, IG2 7HH
Tel: +44 (0)181 599 8866 Fax: +44 (0)181 599 0984
NORTH AMERICA
c/o ISBS, 5804 NE Hassalo Street, Portland OR 97213 3644
Tel: (800) 944 6190 Fax: (503) 280 8832 E-mail: orders@isbs.com
Website: http://www.frankcass.com E-mail: sales@frankcass.com